Hwa Rang Do®
DEFEND · TAKE DOWN · SUBMIT

by Taejoon Lee
with Mark Cheng

Hwa Rang Do®
DEFEND · TAKE DOWN · SUBMIT

by Taejoon Lee
with Mark Cheng

Edited by Raymond Horwitz, Edward Pollard,
Jeannine Santiago and Jon Thibault

Cover Photo by Rick Hustead

Technique Photography by Greg Wetzel

Back Cover Photo by Kal Yee

Graphic Design by John Bodine

The term "hwa rang do" is a registered service mark
of Dr. Joo Bang Lee and the
World Hwa Rang Do Association (WHRDA)

Library of Congress Control Number: 2005924313

ISBN-10: 0-89750-147-0
ISBN-13: 978-0-89750-147-7

Fourth printing 2007

WARNING

BLACK BELT BOOKS
A Division of **OHARA PUBLICATIONS, INC.**
World Leader in Martial Arts Publications

DEDICATIONS

To my father, mentor and teacher, for bringing me into this world and instilling within me the spirit of the Hwarang and for reintroducing the Hwarang knighthood to the world through the founding of *hwa rang do*. Choosing a life of devotion to hwa rang do was my choice, but I must thank my father for instilling within me the strong values and character that have helped me achieve the success I enjoy today. Without his strength, unyielding spirit and, most important, his love, I could not have matured into the teacher I am. As I carry the teachings of hwa rang do around the world and share them on foreign shores, I pray constantly that the legacy I create is one that my father and the generations of Hwarang before him will be proud of.

To the past, present and future Hwarang knights, for their undying devotion and loyalty to their king, country, master and the preservation of their art. May it last another 2,000 years.

Also, I would like to especially thank UCLA law professor Jerry Kang, UCLA network administrator Scott MacKnight, and my loyal and beloved students and disciples, who have inspired me as their teacher and assisted me in making this book a reality.

And to my brother, Mark Cheng, for his selfless devotion to the highest standards of martial brotherhood.

Chief Master Taejoon Lee

To my beloved father, Cheng Yu-Nien, for opening my eyes as a child to the world of martial arts. All the good things in my life have come from my involvement in martial arts training, teaching, researching and writing.

And to my brother, Taejoon Lee, for his unending inspiration, devotion and brotherhood.

These are two men who have opened my eyes, opened my mind and opened my heart.

Sifu Mark J. Cheng, L.Ac.

Chief Master Taejoon Lee (left) and *Sifu* Mark Cheng

ABOUT THE AUTHORS

TAEJOON LEE

Few men are born into martial arts like Taejoon Lee. At the time of his birth in the Korean springtime of the early 1960s, his father was the most visible and most active man in the Korean martial arts scene. A dynamo of leadership, Dr. Joo Bang Lee almost single-handedly brought Korean traditional martial arts out of the dark ages following the Japanese occupation and the Korean War. His first son, Taejoon, was destined to follow in his footsteps.

Photo courtesy WHRDA

Taejoon Lee and his father, Supreme Grandmaster Dr. Joo Bang Lee, in the 1960s

Lee was raised in his father's *dojang*, and his early childhood was filled with training that most other martial artists would envy. While other children were playing outside, he was rolling on the mats with *hwa rang do* masters and learning to perform physical feats that others could only marvel at.

At age 9, Lee came with his family to America. Those early years in the United States presented many challenges to the young Korean immigrant; he had to learn the language and adopt new customs while preserving the heritage of his ancestral homeland. Throughout his school years, Lee also maintained a rigorous schedule as a master instructor of his father's art, managing and teaching at his own dojang at only 16 years old.

As a young adult, Lee was an exemplary member of the Korean-American community. A standout in his academic pursuits, he seemed to be on the fast track to a high-paying job. Instead, he chose not to pursue a modern American career and instead focused all of his energy on the preservation and propagation of his father's legacy—hwa rang do. Lee has boldly ventured into every medium as a means of spreading Korea's most comprehensive martial art, and his influence can be seen in feature films, magazine articles, instructional videos and on the Internet.

At the time of this writing, Lee serves as the vice president of the World Hwa Rang Do Association and holds the position of seventh-degree black sash chief master of the West Coast Hwa Rang Do Academy in Los Angeles. He continues to work tirelessly as the 59th-generation heir to the art of hwa rang do and the traditions of the Hwarang warriors.

MARK J. CHENG

Mark J. Cheng, L.Ac., is a Chinese medicine physician and martial arts researcher based in Los Angeles. Like Taejoon Lee, Cheng began his foray into martial arts with his father, and he later studied with some of the most outstanding masters of Chinese martial arts and medicine. During his undergraduate years as an East Asian studies major, Cheng became fascinated with Korea and immersed himself in the language and culture of China's neighbor. While teaching kung fu at the University of California, Los Angeles, he often crossed paths with Lee, as their martial arts classes held adjacent time slots. Through the years, the two became close friends, and they now consider themselves brothers. This book is a product of that brotherhood.

Cheng serves as a contributing editor to *Black Belt* and writes a monthly column that examines a wide range of traditional martial arts. Cheng is deeply devoted to Chinese martial arts in particular, and he continues his studies as a student and Los Angeles representative of Master David C. K. Lin in the combat system *shuai chiao*. He also practices and teaches southern *sil lum* kung fu and *yang* style *tai chi*. Cheng teaches Chinese *tui na* manual therapeutics at Los Angeles-area Chinese medicine colleges, and he maintains his own successful private clinical practice in Santa Monica, California.

FOREWORD

A silver bullet is an item of curious symbolism in Western culture. Yet if you look at the words "silver" and "bullet" separately and together, they add deeper meaning to the concepts that are being presented to you in this book.

A bullet is a symbol of instant and powerful destruction or death. The slug is the part of the bullet that is launched out of the barrel of the firearm toward the target, and it is traditionally made of some substance containing a high amount of lead. Lead—a cheaply obtained, soft metal that can be easily shaped into small rounds—has adequate density for maintaining momentum in flight toward the target. It also has a poisonous property that increases its effectiveness as an implement of death in those cases when the shot doesn't strike a vital area.

Silver is one of the world's most valuable metals. While it might seem ludicrous to fashion disposable and lethal slugs out of a precious metal, silver bullets maintain a quasi-mystical status. In Western lore, only bullets made from silver can kill a werewolf. Other traditions hold that a silver bullet is truer in flight, keeping a pure line toward its target. Even the Lone Ranger—the American gunslinging hero—fashioned his bullets from silver to remind himself to shoot only when absolutely necessary and to never take a life without sufficient cause (reminiscent of the fifth code of the Hwarang). Medicinally, silver is a bacteriostat, which serves as a means of saving human life.

The silver-bullet concept, as it applies to *hwa rang do*, will give the reader a way to handle the "monster" opponents he or she might encounter. Indeed, the techniques presented here are extremely well-rounded and involve striking, joint manipulation, throwing, grappling and submissions. Just as the primer in a cartridge ignites the gunpowder that propels the bullet, the Stage I defensive techniques presented in this book will give the reader a means to spring into action. The Stage II throwing techniques will show how to channel the force of the initial technique into the takedown, just as the cartridge helps direct the energy from the blasting gunpowder. Finally, the Stage III submission techniques will serve as the finishing moves, reminiscent of a bullet hitting its target. For empty-hand self-defense, this is perhaps your best chance for survival; these techniques will help you develop abilities in any position and from any angle.

Yet the silver bullet must also be wielded with a strong mind and from a true heart, which is why the historical background and essays on the different facets of the Hwarang warrior spirit have been included as a mental and spiritual guide. It would be grossly negligent to dole out combative knowledge such as this without giving the reader an ethical sense of proper conduct. In this way, the reader develops both mind and body into the purest silver bullets. The self becomes the ultimate tool for preserving life.

PREFACE

There is no shortage of martial arts books on the market. This, however, aims to be far more than a simple how-to manual. Owing to the multiplicity of historical and technical issues that this book addresses, some important changes have been made to the conventional format.

Most Korean words, other than proper names with widely accepted spellings (such as President Park Chung-Hee), are spelled using the Mc-Cune-Reischauer Romanization system. Because the historical section of this book holds academic value regarding Korean martial history, we thought it was important to present Korean terms in the manner that scholars would find most familiar. While some readers might be confused by certain spellings, we hope that overall the Korean words used in this text will be easily understood.

In some instances, we opted to use a modification of the McCune-Reischauer system and keep the Romanized syllables separated, sometimes by hyphenation, rather than form a compound word; for example, *nae gong* is used instead of *naegong*. This was done to facilitate the learning of the proper Korean pronunciation. We also decided to keep the phonetically friendlier version of the "shi-" prefix spelled as such, instead of the "si-" spelling that is the McCune-Reischauer standard.

Following the historical and background sections of the text, the technical section of this book is divided into three main parts. The first breaks down the science of joint manipulation into a step-by-step process. Richly illustrated and with detailed explanations, it is presented with as much clarity as possible. The second section shows how one can acquire the same takedown technique, regardless of the manner of attack, and the third demonstrates how to flow into different submissions under different circumstances.

To accomplish this, we have defined three stages of combat, depending on the range of engagement:

Stage I: standing combat from a distance

Stage II: close-range standing combat

Stage III: ground fighting and submissions

Stage I includes six different attacks, and these are used for each of the Stage II joint locks, which take the opponent to the ground. In Stage III, various finishing moves can be applied in order to effectively submit the opponent. With a variety of different attacking scenarios, one who is skilled in these concepts can develop the ability to guide different attacks from different angles into the same joint-manipulation takedown, and then diverge into an assortment of submission techniques.

The technical section of this book is written in a conversational tone. We believe the old saying, "True knowledge is transmitted from the heart by means of the spoken word." While this is far from the "spoken word," we have attempted to give the reader a closer sense of what a private lesson in the West Coast Hwa Rang Do headquarters would be like.

INTRODUCTION

To truly understand the concepts of an art, you must first understand the culture from which it arose. To understand that culture, you must research its history. In researching its history, you must sift through volumes of information in order to extract verifiable facts and corroborated statements.

There is always much discussion within the martial arts community concerning the validity of various claims made by martial arts grandmasters and founders, regardless of their styles or national origins. I do not like to address these issues because I believe that truth should be discovered through personal experience—through research, travel and human interaction—rather than from rumors, gossip and hearsay. Nonetheless, I think it is important to share my truth so that readers can better understand my motivations, my passions and how I arrived at this point in my life. In short, I have come to understand that my life—my truth—is intertwined with the fiber of *hwa rang do*, and that hwa rang do is a crucial thread in the tapestry of Korean martial history.

It is important to understand that the modern Korean martial arts were founded immediately following Korea's freedom from Japanese occupation (1910-1945) and the Korean War (1950-1953), which marked Korea's entrance into the modern industrial age and the birth of what is now South Korea.

Korea in the late 1950s and early 1960s experienced a turbulent "survival of the fittest" period, when actions truly spoke louder and mightier than words. It was a time when government officials had the power to arrest and execute whomever they chose, often for denouncing communism, regardless of the accusation's basis in fact. These were dangerous times for those on both sides of the law. Anyone in a position of power could easily find himself lying in a countryside ditch if rivals or political opponents got the upper hand.

The entire nation was rebuilding its war-torn cities from the ashes and becoming one of the top international economic powers. Korea was frantically trying to rediscover its identity, and the streets were filled with opportunists taking advantage of the country's regained freedom and renewed nationalism. To put it in American terms, it was like the Roaring '20s and the Great Depression rolled into one. Just as American cities in the 1920s are often depicted with scenes of mobsters and bootleggers, bands of gangsters roamed urban Korea in the middle part of the century. The common people were forced to rally against them, defending themselves with their

Chief Master Taejoon Lee and Supreme Grandmaster Dr. Joo Bang Lee

bare hands or whatever everyday implements could be used as weapons. Even today, it is illegal for the public to possess firearms in Korea.

It is owing to this dangerous era that martial arts became a necessity for the common people who chose not to be affiliated with gangs. My father, Dr. Joo Bang Lee, not only developed the most successful chain of martial art schools in Seoul, South Korea, but also protected the public from unruly street thugs. He quickly gained notoriety and respect from the common people and was given the nickname "the man who came down from the mountain."

Korean society and culture were basically defined in Seoul, and the competitive social environment during that period made living there difficult. Seoul was, and still is, the epicenter of all political and social reform, social activity, intellectual study, trendsetting fashion, technological advancement and industrialization. To successfully establish oneself in Seoul meant national recognition, and there was no shortage of martial arts instructors who were struggling to put their schools and their styles in the limelight.

It was in this climate, before *taekwondo* became Korea's national sport, that my father created a vast chain of hwa rang do schools based in Seoul. No other Korean martial arts organization, style or school can claim such a high level of achievement during that time in history. To be the founder of such a martial art, to establish such a successful chain of schools in Seoul, and to accomplish these things in the pressure-filled social, political and economic environment of that period speaks volumes about the man my father was and is.

As I stated in the July 2001 issue of *Black Belt*, "In 1985, there was a Korean martial arts gathering in San Francisco. *Hapkido*, taekwondo and *kuk sool* masters were there. When it came time for the masters to be seated at the head table, Ji Han-Jae, who is revered as the senior-most hapkido practitioner in the world, was given the seat of honor. The older masters know their place with each other. When they come face to face, they know who trained with whom and what each other's secrets are. There's no hiding behind the media or a Web site. I arrived late with my father and my uncle, Joo Sang Lee. When we walked in, Ji Han-Jae got up, as did everyone else, and changed places. My father sat at the seat of honor, followed by Ji Han-Jae and my uncle. That told me everything I needed to know."

Never has my father boasted to me of his skills, his knowledge or his associations. As my father, he needed to prove nothing to me. Only through the stories my mother told me did I learn of my father's early accomplishments and the history he created. It was his ability to never relent, never

Chief Master Taejoon Lee with his disciples, professor Jerry Kang (left) and instructor Scott MacKnight

give in to self-doubt, never give credence to critics, never envy others, and to consistently outperform himself that inspired my lifelong commitment to hwa rang do.

There is no fortune in hwa rang do that I stand to inherit. It is not IBM or Sony or Microsoft; it is not listed in the Fortune 500, nor would it be in the Fortune 10,000 if there were one. I've had opportunities in many other professions that probably would have secured for me a better financial position. However, I was empowered by hwa rang do and its way of life. It made me a better, stronger person, and I realized that it had the power to do the same for other people. I was inspired by my father's passion and his undying perseverance in maintaining the hwa rang do legacy, even in the face of hardship.

I am blessed as a student and a son because my mentor and my father are the same person. Many people know him as a man, a teacher and a martial artist, but only I have known him as a god (when I was young), a father (always) and a mentor (when I became a man). No one is perfect, but of all the great leaders I have had the pleasure of meeting, no one has worked harder than my father. I am constantly searching for mentors, but I have yet to meet one who can inspire me like he has.

The truth never lies in words, pictures, books or Web sites. It lies in your heart. This book is my truth—as I have heard it, as I have researched it, as I have experienced it and as I know it. This is my heart, the essence of hwa rang do. The history in this book isn't mere fable or fiction. The techniques in this book represent the purest essence of hwa rang do's empty-hand combat as I have grown to understand and embody it.

I hope you enjoy the book and gain something of value from it.

Chief Master Taejoon Lee

이태준 李太準

TABLE OF CONTENTS

DEDICATIONS 4

ABOUT THE AUTHORS 6

FOREWORD 8

PREFACE 10

INTRODUCTION 12

PART I – HISTORY

Chapter 1: Korean Martial History 20

Chapter 2: Modern History 35

Chapter 3: Hwa Rang Do 47

Chapter 4: Um-Yang Theory 57

PART II – COMBAT CONCEPTS

Chapter 5: Stages of Fighting 60

Concepts of Joint Manipulation 61

Other Joint-Manipulation Concepts 62

Types of Grips and Arm Control 66

Ground Control 78

PART III - HWA RANG DO IN ACTION

Chapter 6: The Techniques 80

   C-Locks 81

   Outside C-Lock 81

   Two-Hand C-Lock 89

   Inside Circle-Under C-Lock 97

   Outside Reverse C-Lock 104

   Outside Circle-Under Reverse C-Lock 112

Chapter 7: L-Lock 121

Chapter 8: Figure-Four Locks 129

   Inside Figure-Four L-Lock 137

Chapter 9: Wrist-Elbow-Shoulder (WES) Lock 145

   Circle-Under WES 152

Chapter 10: Outside Wrist Twist 160

Chapter 11: S-Lock 168

   Reverse S-Lock 176

Chapter 12: Armbars 184

   Knifehand Armbar 184

   Top Shoulder Armbar 192

   Armpit Armbar 200

   Leg Armbar 209

GLOSSARY 217

PART I – HISTORY

CHAPTER 1

KOREAN MARTIAL HISTORY

FROM THE ORIGINS OF THE KOREAN PEOPLE TO THE END OF THE CHOSON DYNASTY

People tend to think of history as being a black-and-white, clear-cut presentation of facts. Problems arise with the realization that history is more about perspective and interpretation than it is a formulaic timeline, and these perspectives and interpretations are altered by the social, economic and political climate of the period. East Asian martial arts history in particular has always been fraught with controversy and dissent. The records we are left with today have been altered and rewritten by the course of events that played out in China, Japan and Korea, especially during the middle part of the 20th century.

China's long martial arts tradition was almost completely wiped out during Chairman Mao Zedong's Cultural Revolution of the 1970s. Mao claimed that comrades had no business fighting one another in his vision of the perfect Chinese communist state, and he outlawed the practice of traditional Chinese combative arts. Mao's fears were not unfounded; history points to several examples of groups of martial arts practitioners that were instrumental in overthrowing unpopular governments in China. For example, the *Yi He Tuan*, or Boxer Rebellion, was greatly responsible for the decline of the Qing dynasty at the turn of the century. In order to further his own goals and political doctrines, Mao and his Chinese Communist Party rewrote history to portray traditional martial arts as backward, outdated and counterrevolutionary. Many martial arts masters were killed, tortured, jailed or "re-educated" to ensure that their thoughts fell along party lines.

Korean history was also revised, but not by its own government. When the Japanese Empire had begun its expansionist movement at the turn of the century, Korea was the closest victim. The Korean peninsula was a prized military possession because it served as the perfect springboard into the Chinese mainland. The Japanese punished the Chinese in the Sino-Japanese War of 1894 and forced them to relinquish Korea's status as a Chinese tributary and protectorate, which left it vulnerable to Japan's subsequent invasion.

While the official dates of Japan's Korean occupation are 1910 to 1945, the actual incursion started 15 years earlier. By the time the occupation was in full swing, the Japanese set about rewriting Korean history with a decidedly colonial tone.

This sort of cultural subjugation is meant to breed compliance among the oppressed by teaching them that they are inferior to their oppressors. The practice of Korean martial arts was completely outlawed and made a capital offense, as were many other facets of Korean culture. Korean historical documents were destroyed as well, further obscuring Korea's place in the history of East Asia for generations to come.

As a result of these tragedies, many Korean martial arts schools either unwittingly propagated some of these Japanese lies or fabricated ultra-nationalistic histories that denied the influence of Japanese martial arts altogether. Another factor that contributed to the haziness of Korea's history was the language barrier that many masters faced during the post-war diaspora. As these masters settled in different countries, they spread their arts to new audiences, but they were not always able to answer historical questions with any academic accuracy; students recorded their interpretations of what their masters had said in broken tongues, and more misconceptions were fostered and spread through the print media.

Hwa rang do, as part of the Korean martial art landscape, has also been forced to deal with inaccuracies regarding its history. Fortunately, thanks to a new generation of multicultural historians who are educated in East Asian history, languages, cultures and medicine, we are pleased to bring you the definitive history of hwa rang do. While we do not intend this to be a comprehensive study of Korean history, we hope that the following section clarifies the development of different martial arts during the course of Korea's evolution.

Early unarmed combat skills are referred to by many names in Korean historical texts. Perhaps the most common is *su-bak*, which means "hand fighting" or "unarmed combat." Many historians and martial arts instructors wrongly assume that su-bak is a distinct style, when it is actually a generic term that was used by the Chinese (*shou-bo*) much earlier in history—as far back as the Qin dynasty (221-206 B.C.).

The same can be said of the Korean term *kwon-bop*, the literal translation of which is "fist method." Kwon-bop does not refer to a specific style. Traditionally, *kwon* (or *quan* in Chinese) is a generic term for a martial art, and it encompasses unarmed fighting techniques, weaponry training, and sometimes energy-cultivation exercises. For example, *Cholla Nam-Do kwon* refers to any or all of the different martial arts practiced in Cholla

21

Nam-Do, and *Hwarang-kwon* refers to any combative training that the Hwarang practiced. Likewise, Chinese *Shaolin quan* refers to the martial art of the Shaolin Temple, and *taijiquan* refers to the martial art under the philosophical banner of *tai chi chuan*. To say that people practiced su-bak or kwon-bop is correct in a generic sense, but to assert that they practiced a specific martial art called su-bak or kwon-bop is incorrect. This distinction is very important when trying to understand Korean martial art history.

Contrary to popular belief, early Korean combat systems were not taught in a systematized, curriculum-driven manner. The earliest combat instructors were individuals who earned government recognition by demonstrating their combat skills in village festivals. These were not trained martial artists but rather simple men who were proficient in armed or unarmed combat. As government employees, they taught the legions to which they were assigned and imparted the skills necessary for leadership. Early chieftains were those who distinguished themselves as being wise enough, strong enough and fierce enough to assume the role of leadership and protect their fellow tribesmen.

ORIGINS OF THE KOREAN PEOPLE: KO CHOSON

Hand-to-hand combat is as old as humankind, and the different fighting styles that prevailed in different regions of the world evolved over generations. Individual countries, kingdoms and tribes developed their own particular combat skills in order to protect their people and their way of life. Combat-skill sets are thus indicative of variances in culture.

Korean combat skills began evolving some 5,000 years ago, when T'an-gun Wang-gom established the kingdom of Ko Choson by unifying six tribes in the northern part of the Korean peninsula. Ko Choson established a strong warrior tradition, and its territory quickly spread far from the original peninsula, eventually including all of Manchuria and, according to some accounts, a great deal of China.

Ko Choson's expansion attracted the unfavorable attention of the Chinese Han dynasty's Emperor Wu, whose armies invaded and conquered the kingdom in the second century B.C. Nevertheless, the long history and expansion of Ko Choson is a testament to the combative ability of its warriors and the fighting spirit of its people.

THE THREE KINGDOMS: KOGURYO, PAEKCHE AND SILLA

After the fall of Ko Choson, Chinese traders, soldiers and colonists made their way onto the peninsula, marking the era of greatest Chinese influence on Korea's people. A new era was about to dawn. One of the tribal conglomerates on the northern part of the peninsula blossomed into a full-fledged kingdom. They pushed the Chinese out and expanded into Manchuria, creating the Koguryo kingdom, which lasted from 37 B.C. to 668 A.D.

Koguryo's warrior corps, known as *Sonbae*, played a crucial role in the consolidation of Koguryo's power in its formative years. They were known for their incredible fighting spirit and were never afraid to engage the Chinese in battle. The term "sonbae" has survived in modern Korean language and indicates a superior in the armed forces, workplace, school or any other institution. The term was also adopted in Japan, where it is spelled *senpai*.

Photo courtesy WHRDA; artifacts photographed at Kyungbok Palace Museum in Seoul, South Korea

The traditional wardrobe of the king and queen of Koguryo

The Paekche kingdom (18 B.C.-660 A.D.) appeared shortly after the establishment of Koguryo. Founded by people fleeing the aggressiveness of the new Koguryo kingdom, Paekche resided on the southern end of the peninsula to avoid trouble. The quiet kingdom established strong trade relations with China but was not without its own military ambitions. It expanded into Japan in 369 A.D., from Hakata Bay all the way to the Yamato plain at Osaka Bay.

The Paekche invaders were the progenitors of the Yamato kingdom of Japan. Paekche Prince Homuda declared himself the first Yamato king in 390 A.D., and his Paekchean expatriates became entrenched in their newfound home, flooding the Yamato and Nara areas and subsuming the local culture. Through it all, Paekche maintained strong relations with the new territory.

Photo courtesy WHRDA; artifacts photographed at Kyungbok Palace Museum in Seoul, South Korea

The traditional wardrobe of the king and queen of Paekche

According to some legends, as the Ko Choson period drew toward its end, the six chieftains of the six tribes unified by T'an-gun Wang-gom were highly disturbed by the absence of a strong leader who could maintain order over their people. Lamenting the state of affairs, they met to lay the plans for a new kingdom, and they pooled their knowledge of combat skills, cultural wisdom and esoteric arts to develop a potential head of state. The chieftains passed their cumulative knowledge on to the man who later became the founder of the Silla kingdom, Pak Hyokkose.

Silla (57 B.C.-935 A.D.) was geographically and ideologically the farthest from China, making it the "most Korean" of the three kingdoms. Situated in the southeast of the peninsula, Silla was the late bloomer of the bunch, in that it was the last to adopt any Chinese cultural influences, but it was probably the first to emphasize comprehensive combat training. It was in Silla that the Hwarang knights were born.

The traditional wardrobe of the king and queen of Silla

Photo courtesy WHRDA; artifacts photographed at Kyungbok Palace Museum in Seoul, South Korea

   The book *Hwarang Segi* ("Annals of Hwarang"), which chronicled the Hwarang and their exploits, did not survive past the 12th century. The *Samguk Sagi* ("Chronicles of the Three Kingdoms") is the oldest Korean historical text in existence; it features excerpts from and references to the *Hwarang Segi* but does not include it in its entirety. As a result, the roots of the Hwarang are shrouded in mystery. There is little doubt, however, that the Hwarang were heirs to generations of accumulated combat skills from the Ko Choson period.

   In ancient times, there was no clear codification of combat or leadership skills but rather a comprehensive education gathered from different sources (exemplified by Pak Hyokkose). This cooperative effort to develop political and military leaders who were outstanding in every facet of life and society would later be called the Hwarang movement.

Photo courtesy WHRDA; artifacts photographed at National Independence Museum in Seoul, South Korea

Chief Master Taejoon Lee stands before a model of a Hwarang warrior.

FROM MOVEMENT TO INSTITUTION: THE HWARANG CORPS

Around 570 A.D., King Chinhung of Silla issued an edict for the organization of a formalized military. Instead of trying to recruit men with martial arts talent, he decided to develop warriors from childhood. This elite group was called the Hwarang Corps. While some elects came from lower classes, they were by far the exceptions because the corps was comprised mostly of youths of noble birth. The royal court selected young men based on their mental talents and their genetic gifts of strength, stature and physical beauty. They represented the finest of Silla's young noblemen who, once chosen, were guided toward the pinnacle of human achievement.

The predominantly aristocratic origin of the Hwarang warriors is an important point to keep in mind when trying to translate their title to English. The Chinese character for *hwa* is translated as "flower" or "flowering." Some detractors have made claims that the Hwarang Corps were nothing but a jolly group of aristocratic Sillan boys who roamed the mountains and sang songs to each other, but such statements show a lack of proper research, insight and context.

King Chinhung was devoutly Buddhist, and his choice of words to label his new corps of knights reflected the symbolism of his religious beliefs. The lotus flower represents purity, divinity and enlightenment in Buddhist art, and King Chinhung envisioned the Hwarang Corps as an assembly of Silla's finest young men who embodied those traits. He saw them as the Buddhist ideal of young, patriotic leaders, growing into manhood as enlightened beings.

The *rang* character in "Hwarang" is sometimes translated as "young man," "groom" or "noble." While the modern usage of the word can refer to a young man or groom, the archaic usage unquestionably reflected nobility. Thus, the best translation for the term "hwarang" would be "flowering noble." This carries the meaning of a young nobleman who, with the help of very comprehensive training, blossoms into Sillan society as a leader who is admirable in all ways—physical, mental, emotional and spiritual.

The Hwarang youths followed the instructions of the Buddhist monk Won-Kwang, as laid out in his Five Precepts:

1. *Sa kun yi ch'ung*: Loyalty to your lord and country
2. *Sa ch'in yi hyo*: Obedience to your parents
3. *Kyo u yi shin*: Trustworthiness and goodness among friends
4. *Im chon mu t'oe*: No retreat in battle
5. *Sal saeng yu t'aek*: Discrimination in the taking of life

These Five Precepts became the Hwarang code, and each member of the corps worked diligently to live their lives by these moral and ethical standards.

Along with this base of ethical indoctrination, Hwarang training was designed to address every area of human experience. The corps traveled to remote locations that were renowned for their natural beauty and geomantic powers. Surrounded by lakes, streams, rivers, mountains, forests and other picturesque scenery, the Hwarang were able to train with natural inspiration and in relative seclusion, far away from the distractions of city life and the royal court.

In these settings, the Hwarang fully developed all aspects of their human potential under the guidance of Silla's most outstanding masters in many different arts and sciences. As fighters, they were trained in every possible

Photo courtesy WHRDA

The modern Hwarang visit the training grounds of the ancient Hwarang at the Pulguska (temple).

manner of combat, both unarmed and with more than 100 different weapons. There are many stories of their physical prowess—tales of jumping spin kicks that could dismount a charging cavalryman and punches that could penetrate densely lacquered wooden armor. Their training consisted of techniques that perfectly blended hard and soft, straight and circular, *um* and *yang*.

As scholars who were well-versed in science and classical literature, and as deeply creative artists, the highly educated Hwarang are credited with countless works of literary, scenic and calligraphic art. Many also credit the Hwarang with the creation of *hyang'ga*, a form of Korean poetry that came into existence during the Silla kingdom. Performing arts, such as song and dance, were also practiced.

Other, more spiritual skills were also part of the Hwarang education. They were taught healing techniques that used implements, herbal medicine and their own hands. Spirituality was cultivated through deep meditation and careful practice, which gave the most skilled Hwarang supernatural powers. Their training could be considered the finest blend of China's highest schools of thought—Confucian ethics, Buddhist scripture and Taoist

mysticism—combined with indigenous Korean shamanistic practices, all of which made the Hwarang outstanding leaders and strategists.

The Hwarang Corps was known collectively as the *Hwarang-do*, with *do* meaning "disciples" or "followers." Within the Hwarang-do, there evolved three main rank designations:

1. *Kukson*—These men were the highest level Hwarang. They held the rank of head general, or *Tae Jang-gun* in Korean. Kukson literally means "national immortal" and refers to one who has almost supernatural skills and represents the Silla kingdom.

2. Hwarang—The Hwarang functioned as battlefield leaders or lower-level generals who were under the command of the Kukson and the king. The Hwarang received their training from several different masters under the sponsorship of the Silla royal court. By all accounts, there was no single instructor for the Hwarang in any facet of their education, and Hwarang from one locale may have learned an entirely different set of fighting techniques than another group of Hwarang. While the techniques may have differed in practice, they were all designed to maximize the physical potential of the Hwarang and establish their dominance on the battlefield.

3. *Rangdo*—Literally "disciples of the (Hwa) Rang nobles," the Rangdo was a group of 500 to 5,000 troops of non-noble birth assigned to a particular Hwarang general. Each Hwarang general served as the master instructor to his troops and passed on his particular body of knowledge and special skills to his followers.

UNIFIED SILLA AND THE LEGENDARY GEN. KIM YU-SHIN

With such an elite group of young Renaissance soldiers, Silla evolved to become much more than the late bloomer among the Three Kingdoms. Through centuries of refinement and constant improvements in strategy, battlefield technology, martial skills and mystical training, the Hwarang Corps developed into an almost unstoppable force, poised for conquest.

In 660, the time had come for Silla to make its move. King Munmu ordered the Kukson Gen. Kim Yu-shin to lead the Sillan armies in conquest of Paekche. The Chinese, believing that Silla's armies were strong enough to subdue the other two kingdoms, made an alliance with Silla, and Kim attacked with the help of the Chinese Tang armies. This gave the Sillan

Photos courtesy WHRDA

Chief Master Taejoon Lee (right) and Sifu Mark Cheng in front of Gen. Kim Yu-shin's memorial.

forces a tremendous advantage by allowing them to attack their enemies with a pincer formation—Silla from the south and China from the north. By the end of 668, Kim completed his conquest of the Korean peninsula with the defeat of Koguryo. Although loyalists to the fallen kingdoms remained on the peninsula, the Unified Silla period had begun.

(From left) Chief Master Taejoon Lee, Dr. Joo Bang Lee, Grandmaster Ki Nam Yum and hwa rang do students pay their respects to Gen. Kim Yu-shin.

Following the victories against Paekche and Koguryo, the Chinese turned on Silla, hoping to make an easy conquest against the newly unified and war-weary peninsula. But the Silla kingdom's Hwarang-based military system was so mighty that they repelled the takeover attempt by the imperial armies of Tang China. Legend has it that, during one argument with a Chinese general, Kim's sword unsheathed itself and leapt into his hand. Because the sword was regarded as an extension of the warrior's soul, the sight filled the Chinese general with such fear that he apologized to Kim. Such tales of mastery and rousing victories raised the morale and conviction of the Hwarang Corps to even higher levels and elevated their reputation to almost mythical proportions in the eyes of both their foes and the common folk.

Photo courtesy WHRDA

The cliff where 3,000 Paekchean concubines leapt to their death rather than face capture by invading Sillans.

THE FALL OF SILLA AND THE BIRTH OF KORYO

By 935, Silla, like so many monarchies and dynasties, had fallen to disarray and corruption. Courtiers and courtesans were embroiled in power brokering, and generals struggled to defend the kingdom from outside forces while defending themselves from domestic conspirators.

Some of the Sillan noble families fled to Japan after the fall of their kingdom. Shinra Saburo, the founder of Japanese *daito-ryu jujutsu*, was most likely of Korean ancestry, as his name illustrates. *Shinra* is the Japanese pronunciation of "Silla," and *Saburo* means "third noble" or "third gentleman."

The Hwarang influence was also exported to Japan. The shogun and samurai systems are said to have evolved from the example set by the Hwarang Corps. Shogun is the Japanese pronunciation of the Korean word *chang-gun* (meaning "general"), and the shogun commanded legions of samurai warriors, each of whom was trained in what closely resembled the Hwarang system. The Japanese training, however, was more streamlined than the all-encompassing Korean training. While the Hwarang were proficient with all manner of weapons and in empty-handed combat, the samurai learned to use only a few different weapons and even fewer un-armed techniques. It was this focused and streamlined training that elevated Japanese swordsmanship.

In 936, King T'aejo of Koguryo, a former Hwarang general, rose up and defeated the remaining Paekche and Silla loyalists and assumed total control of the Korean peninsula. King T'aejo (also known as Wang Kon), christened his new kingdom the Koryo dynasty, and it lasted until 1392. During that time, the Hwarang institution continued on, but under different titles, such as the *Kukson-do* (the National Immortal Corps) and *P'ungwol-do* (the Wind-Moon Corps). Though the labels changed, the Hwarang legacy remained remarkably intact during the Koryo dynasty.

CHOSON: THE DECLINE OF THE HWARANG

In 1392, another Hwarang general, Yi Song-gye, overthrew Koryo and created the Choson kingdom (not to be confused with the ancient Ko Choson kingdom), the last ruling dynasty of Korea. Also known as the Yi (or Lee) dynasty, the Choson kingdom lasted until 1910. It was during this period that Korean martial arts began their decline.

Yi set out to create a Confucian state in Choson and required the new government officials to be educated in Confucian-style academies. Orthodox Confucianism placed extreme emphasis on social hierarchy, and the military had no place in it. Although the Hwarang were the product of Buddhist Silla, three of their five codes were distinctly Confucian, and only the fifth code had a Buddhist flavor. Nonetheless, the new aristocracy began to look at the martial pursuits of the Hwarang with condescending eyes.

In 1401, Yi's son T'aejong became the third king of Choson. He destroyed the Hwarang system by initiating a policy that, among other things, placed all Rangdo soldiers under his sole control. Knowing how his father had achieved hegemony, King T'aejong feared the power of the individual Hwarang generals, many of whom still held strong ties with their native villages. With this grass-roots power base, each Hwarang general posed a potential threat to his reign. King T'aejong believed that the possibility of a Hwarang attack was great, and he issued an edict that effectively stripped the generals of their rank, title and troops. Had his father not converted Choson to a Confucian education system, King T'aejong probably would not have had such an easy time disposing of the Hwarang.

Choson still maintained a military to protect its borders (the government later compiled the *Muye Dobo T'ongji*—a canonical text that catalogued empty-hand and weapons techniques), but the new centralization placed all aspects of the military under tight control of the king, rendering the existence of the Hwarang Corps and the Kukson-Hwarang leadership unnecessary. King T'aejong's edict forced many of the Hwarang to flee into the mountains and other remote places in Korea. They lived like wandering hermits, devoting themselves to spiritual study while secretly passing on their vast knowledge of religion, combat skills and healing techniques to a select few disciples instead of huge bands of Rangdo.

These Hwarang masters occasionally accepted new students when a suitable candidate came along, but if a master did not find a worthy student, he simply kept his skills to himself and took his wisdom to the grave. With the passing of time and the advancement of the Choson dynasty, a great deal of traditional Hwarang skills gradually died out forever, but many of their remarkable techniques and traditions were successfully passed from monks to their successors, and the Hwarang legacy survived into the 20th century.

CHAPTER 2

MODERN HISTORY

THE DARK AGES

In 1910, shortly after the Chinese were defeated in the Sino-Japanese War, the Choson dynasty fell into Japanese hands, and the Japanese occupation of Korea began. The occupation, which lasted until 1945, was disastrous for Korea in all respects, not just for its martial arts. All aspects of its culture were subjected to a strict revision process; Koreans were forced to speak Japanese in public, dress in the Japanese manner, and act and think like Japanese in almost every way. The observance of Korean traditions was banned and carried the penalty of incarceration, torture or death. Traditional Korean dress, spoken language, *han'gul* writing, martial arts and even Korean names were outlawed. The Japanese obliterated countless historical archives, libraries and records—stripping the Koreans of their past—and attempted to rewrite Korean history in a manner that portrayed them as historically, culturally and biologically inferior to the Japanese.

The martial arts were already in decline during the later years of the Choson dynasty owing to King T'aejong's decree, but the Japanese occupation almost completely destroyed what little still remained in the public eye. Martial arts instructors who chose to publicly practice were forced to learn and teach Japanese martial arts, such as *shotokan* karate, judo and *kendo*. Korean martial arts history was written in Japanese during these dark years, and the light shined again only with the defeat of the Japanese at the end of World War II.

CHOI YONG-SUL: A JAPANESE ART TAKES ROOT IN KOREAN SOIL

During the occupation, Choi Yong-Sul, the Korean man often credited with founding *hapkido*, served as a house servant for one of the last great Japanese martial arts masters, Takeda Sokaku. Takeda was the headmaster of the daito-ryu jujutsu, or *yawara* system ("yawara" is generally acknowledged as being an older term for jujutsu). Choi was taken from Korea to Japan during the occupation (some say he was kidnapped) and lived there for some three decades with Takeda. During his time in the Takeda household, Choi was constantly exposed to martial arts training and even served as Takeda's personal assistant in his teaching duties.

When the occupation ended, Choi returned to Korea. He brought back scrolls recording his place in the daito-ryu lineage from Takeda himself, but he lost his bags to a thief during the trip. Upset by the loss of such important documents, Choi's return to Korea was not initially pleasant, and he soon found himself working at menial labor jobs to survive. The absence of the scrolls gave some historians grounds to question Choi's legitimacy in the daito-ryu lineage, but an analysis of the techniques practiced by Choi's students shows a clear link to the techniques of daito-ryu.

A judo player named So Bok-Sop was the first person to "discover" Choi after his return. One day, So was lounging around in a loft at his father's *makkolli* (liquor) brewery on his family's property. During that time, pig farmers used brewed grains for pig feed, thereby disposing of the brewery's refuse. A man came in with a wheelbarrow to get some free pig feed, and a scuffle ensued between him and some local troublemakers. Hearing the commotion, So looked down from the loft and was amazed to see the man break the thugs' joints and send them flying.

As soon as his assailants were subdued, the man picked up the wheelbarrow and started walking away. So jumped down from the loft and sprinted after him to find out what incredible martial art he practiced. The man pushing the wheelbarrow was Choi, and after much persuasion, he accepted So as his first Korean student. In 1953, after the Korean War, Choi opened his first public school in his home and called his art *taedong-ryu yusul*—the Korean pronunciation of daito-ryu jujutsu.

Choi would become one of the great fathers of Korean martial arts during its period of rebirth. He kept his Japanese system intact and remained loyal to Takeda's teachings, including his philosophy that the immediate neutralization of one's opponent was only a small part of the art. This explains the rougher nature of Choi's locking and throwing techniques in comparison to those of another daito-ryu offshoot, *aikido*.

DR. JOO BANG LEE:
A FLOWER BLOOMS IN THE WINTER OF JAPANESE OCCUPATION

Born in what is now North Korea during the late 1930s, Dr. Joo Bang Lee began his study of martial arts with his father, Ha-Young Lee. Ha-Young Lee had studied Japanese judo and kendo during the Japanese occupation, and because Korea remained a dangerous place, he believed it was imperative that his children study self-defense as soon as they could walk on their own.

Seeing his son's physical aptitude and strong desire to learn martial arts,

Ha-Young Lee took Joo Bang Lee and his older brother, Joo Sang Lee, to the Sok-Wang Temple. The temple was the home of Su-Am Dosa, a friend of Ha-Young Lee's. He asked Su-Am Dosa to accept his sons as his students and make them his sole disciples. At the time of their acceptance in 1942, Joo Bang Lee was 4 years old and Joo Sang Lee was 5.

Dosa means "master of the way." Su-Am Dosa was the 57th-generation heir to a lineage of Hwarang training handed down from the Silla period. Until he accepted the young Lee brothers as his students, he had not shared his knowledge with others. Su-Am Dosa, like the masters before him, would have been completely content to take his wisdom to the grave in the absence of a worthy disciple. He referred to the martial section of his teachings as *um-yang kwon*. In Chinese, *um-yang* is pronounced "yin-yang," and the term referred to the hard-soft nature of his balanced body of knowledge.

The Lee brothers trained almost daily with their Hwarang master, waking at 5 a.m., washing with cold mountain water, warming up and training for an hour, making breakfast and serving Su-Am Dosa, cleaning up by 8 a.m., training with Su-Am Dosa for three or four hours, cooking and eating lunch, napping for an hour at 1 p.m., training for another four hours under their master's strict eye, and then cooking dinner. After the dinner bowls were cleaned, Su-Am Dosa taught the Lee brothers *shin gong* (mental skills), and *in sul* techniques (ancient healing methods).

Their training each day amounted to eight or nine hours of um-yang kwon combat skills, followed by another two or three hours of mental and medical training. Hwarang combat skills were not organized in a systematic belt-by-belt fashion like modern martial arts. It was a continuous training process that created true enjoyment of the journey itself rather than a single-minded focus on attaining a rank.

Su-Am Dosa taught the Lee brothers to develop their ability in kicking, punching, jumping, falling, bone and joint breaking, submission locking, choking, grappling, acrobatic leaping, throwing, pressure-point striking and pressing, and *ki* energy training. Learning hard and soft *hyung* was also part of their regimen, as was instruction in the stealth techniques used by ancient Hwarang spies, known as *sulsa*. There were 260 technical categories with more than 4,000 techniques, along with 108 traditional weapons broken down into 20 categories.

SOUTHERN DISCOMFORT:
THE KOREAN WAR AND SOUTHWARD RELOCATION

In 1948, after the start of the Korean War, the Lee family and Su-Am Dosa fled southward from the communists and relocated to Seoul. Su-Am Dosa made his new home on O-Dae mountain and lived in solitude. It is important to understand that Asian monks, to develop their mental skills without the distractions of the secular world, often prefer lives of solitude instead of spending years in a monastery filled with other monks. The Lee brothers still trained with him daily, however, until their family relocated farther south, to Taegu, in 1950.

It was in Taegu that the Lee brothers met the formidable Choi Yong-Sul. Unable to travel back and forth to Seoul to train daily with Su-Am Dosa, they continued their martial arts development with Choi's taedong-ryu yusul. Unlike the majority of his students, Choi taught the Lee brothers privately because their family could afford the high cost of his lessons. With the benefit of their prior martial arts training with Su-Am Dosa, they were able to comprehend and digest Choi's techniques with ease. In 1956, the Lee brothers received their master-level rankings in yusul from Choi, and their family moved back up to Seoul.

THE BIRTH OF HAPKIDO

Like Choi, Morihei Uyeshiba, the founder of aikido, also studied with Takeda Sokaku. When aikido (meaning "way of harmonious energy") crystallized into a separate martial art in Japan, Korea had cut off diplomatic ties and the Korean yusul practitioners were unaware of Uyeshiba's new art.

According to an interview with Joo Bang Lee in *Black Belt*, a yusul instructor named Kang Mun-Jin read a Japanese aikido text that had somehow made its way into Korea. The Chinese characters that are pronounced "aikido" in Japanese are pronounced "hapkido" in Korean. Kang recognized the similarities between yusul and aikido, and he began using the term "hapkido" for his school in 1959. Choi never gave Kang permission to refer to his teachings as hapkido, however, and believing it was a breach of protocol, he removed the signboard from Kang's school and closed it down. Joo Bang Lee is quoted as saying, "Regardless of how it came about, I know that [Kang] was the very first to use the term 'hapkido' in Korea."

By 1961, Joo Bang Lee and two other yusul practitioners named Ji Han-Jae and Kim Mu-Hong had each opened hapkido schools in Seoul, making them the founding fathers of the hapkido movement. At his Seoul academy, Joo Bang Lee taught Hwarang techniques and changed the banner of the school to hwa rang do ("way of the Hwarang"), much to the dismay of Su-Am Dosa, who had advised him to make a living as an Oriental medicine physician and teach Hwarang combat skills only to his sons. But with the booming popularity of his new academy, Joo Bang Lee could only partially obey his master's request, eventually earning a degree in Eastern medicine from Dong Yang University and serving as a healer in Seoul.

In the winter of 1962, a meeting of seven major yusul practitioners was called. Among them were Joo Bang Lee, Joo Sang Lee, and a yusul and kung fu practitioner named Suh In-Hyuk. These seven charter members founded the first national hapkido organization in Korea, the Korean Martial Arts Association. The Lee brothers worked assiduously to promote martial arts in Korea. Year after year, the popularity of their school blossomed and branch schools spread throughout Seoul. They organized and performed in annual martial arts tournaments and televised expositions at the Jang Chung Sports Arena, and the events further boosted the popularity of Choi's teachings and their own hwa rang do. Many archival photos show the floor of the arena covered with students in hwa rang do uniforms.

The Korean Martial Arts Association dissolved in 1966. By 1967, the Lee brothers' popularity had gained the favorable attention of President Park Chung-Hee. *Taekwondo*, *tang soo do* and *kong soo do* had already been unified two years earlier under the taekwondo banner, and Park's goal was

Photo courtesy WHRDA

Yong-Sul Choi, performing at the Korean Hwa Rang Do Association-sponsored expo in Jang Chung Sports Arena, 1968.

39

to make two unique organizations, one for martial sports and the other for martial arts. He ordered Ji Han-Jae, Joo Bang Lee and others to unify all the Korean martial arts under one organization, the Korean Martial Way Association, which was accountable to the central government.

The crowning moment in Joo Bang Lee's career as a national martial arts policymaker came in 1968 at the Korean National Martial Arts Tournament and Exposition. This event marked the first cooperative effort of Korean martial artists from a wide variety of styles and backgrounds, all performing under one roof. It was a tremendous success and was watched by the entire nation on television. During the exposition, Choi awarded Ji Han-Jae and the Lee brothers eighth-degree black belts in recognition of their skill and dedication. At the time, it was the highest rank ever awarded by Choi. Choi also publicly announced that he would accept the name hapkido for his art.

Looking back on that moment, Joo Bang Lee said, "Once we'd accomplished what we needed to with hapkido—taking it from the countryside and popularizing it in the capital city, earning high masters' rankings, and promoting the art and Master Choi in front of the president of Korea—I knew that our work was good." Later that year, he was awarded the prestigious Lion's Award for Martial Excellence, Korea's highest honor for a martial artist.

Dr. Joo Bang Lee (center) during an outdoor training session with hwa rang do masters in Seoul, South Korea, circa 1960.

DISILLUSIONMENT AND A RETURN TO THE HWARANG ARTS

Despite the earnest efforts of Joo Bang Lee and many others, egos and infighting undercut the unification effort, and the Korean Martial Way Association fell apart. With its dissolution, two new factions were left in

Photo courtesy WHRDA

its place: Joo Bang Lee's Korean Hwa Rang Do Association and the Korean Hapkido Association. The Korean Hapkido Association made a tactical error by selling the rights to hapkido, resulting in the establishment of many different subdivisions of the art. This caused the widespread dilution of hapkido's true science as Choi had taught it, and it made quality control impossible to legally enforce. With this embarrassing turn of events, Park took a strong liking to taekwondo, which he later established as the national sport.

Late in 1968, Joo Bang Lee, disgusted at both the lack of cooperation among the Korean martial arts masters and Park's growing favoritism toward taekwondo, returned to O-Dae mountain to seek the advice of his master, Su-Am Dosa. Explaining both his achievements and his profound heartbreak, Joo Bang Lee told of his dreams to bring the finest Korean martial art knowledge to the Korean people and eventually spread it throughout the world. Instead of berating the ambitious young man, Su-Am Dosa had a change of heart. Surprisingly, he consented and gave Joo Bang Lee his blessing to bring his ancient Hwarang combat skills to the public.

Joo Bang Lee and his brother set out to categorize all the techniques they had learned from Su-Am Dosa, breaking them down into a clear curriculum and belt-sash ranking system for students and instructors to follow. Joo Bang Lee also registered hwa rang do as a martial art identity with the Korean federal government. This gave hwa rang do international trademark protection to ensure that it would not follow the same path as hapkido, and it solidified its status as a separate and unique martial art.

41

In July 1969, Su-Am Dosa passed away. Before his death, he passed on to Joo Bang Lee the title of 58th-.generation Hwarang, making him the supreme grandmaster of hwa rang do. By 1972, Joo Bang Lee had 16 schools in Seoul alone, and 68 schools spread around Korea.

TRANSPLANTING A KOREAN FLOWER TO AMERICAN SOIL

Coming to America was the next logical step in the evolution of hwa rang do. Joo Bang Lee knew that leaving Korea would be a monumental task. He would have to start all over in a country with completely different cultural and historical underpinnings, a place where hwa rang do was completely

unknown. Despite this immense hurdle, America's position as the strongest country in the world made it the ideal base of operations from which to spread hwa rang do to the rest of the world.

In July 1972, Joo Bang Lee left Korea and brought his family to the United States. His brother, Joo Sang

Four-year-old Taejoon Lee poses in a ssang-gum stance, preparing for an uncertain future in America.

Lee, had already moved in 1968 and established the first hwa rang do school in Los Angeles. The language barrier was immense and created misinformation about hwa rang do and its place in Korean martial arts history. Cultural barriers also inhibited the smooth transmission of the art's true history to American students in those early years.

Nevertheless, Joo Bang Lee persisted and opened the World Hwa Rang Do Association headquarters in Downey, California. Soon, the Lee brothers established a medical practice after earning their state board licenses. Joo Bang Lee also earned his doctorate degree in Oriental medicine, putting Su-Am Dosa's Hwarang healing arts to use and serving the people of his new homeland as both a physician and professor. With a flourishing medical practice and martial arts academy, the brothers still found time to teach a version of their art to the U.S. Special Forces through the late Michael Echanis, one of the most respected hand-to-hand military tacticians in the world.

In addition to the numerous hwa rang do schools in the United States, there are now schools in Hong Kong, the Philippines, Denmark, Germany,

Photo courtesy WHRDA

With strength of character nothing is impossible. When your heart expands to embrace the impossible, you are able to lead with Tao.
—*Lao Tzu*

Mexico, Canada, Poland and several other countries. Currently, Asia, Europe and the Americas all have hwa rang do representation.

TAEJOON LEE: BREATHING LIFE INTO THE NEXT GENERATION

I began my journey in life and self-discovery in a small, worn-down *dojang* in Seoul. From my very first breath, my destiny was etched into the fiber of my being. My early memories are almost exclusively centered around martial arts and my father's hwa rang do.

While other children were out playing, I spent my earliest years on the mats. I can clearly recall seeing my father's master-level students performing feats of remarkable athleticism, running up walls and firing off spinning kicks. I mused at how dirty even the ceiling had become with footprints. While other children were taught that weapons were dangerous, I learned to wield them in a way that was beautiful to watch. While other children learned to fear the power of adults, I was taught to respect the adults who conducted themselves with dignity and defend myself against those who did not.

When we moved to the United States, I understood for the first time what racism meant. I never knew that a 9-year-old could be discriminated against because of the color of his skin—something I could not alter even if I wanted to. During the assimilation process, I often felt bitter and angry that my father brought us to America. As I began to understand and real-

Photos courtesy WHRDA

Dojoonim executes a 540-degree hwa rang do spin kick, breaking a board over 10 feet in the air, circa 1960.

ize my potential as a human being—not Korean, not white, not colored—I became empowered through education and hwa rang do.

It was at this point in my youth that I realized that a person must be strong both in mind and body. Without advances in both areas of one's life, true confidence and empowerment cannot be possible. First, you must gain the insight and perspective to know what you want, and then you must attain the power and abilities to achieve your goals. A human being is neither all mind nor all body but rather a single, coordinated unit—an intricate orchestration of both. With this realization, I started to train intensely in hwa rang do as well as excel in my academic pursuits.

In high school, I started a hwa rang do club and also instructed a physical-education class. Mandatory assemblies were held annually, and the power of hwa rang do was demonstrated in front of the entire student body. Along with these commitments, I managed and taught at my own dojang, located in Laguna Hills, California. Hwa rang do and education were my life.

After graduating from high school, I entered college with the goal of becoming a lawyer, working to fulfill my father's wishes. He thought this would be the most beneficial to hwa rang do. I still maintained my hwa rang do training, however, in conjunction with my education. As a freshman at the University of Southern California, I again established a hwa rang do club, and teaching highly motivated people with a great aptitude for learning was an awesome experience. From there, I proceeded to establish the Intercollegiate Hwa Rang Do Society, and hwa rang do clubs were soon created at the University of California, Los Angeles; UC Irvine; UC Riverside; UC San Diego and California State University, Long Beach. It was at this time that I realized the truth in what I had learned earlier: Intellectual study and martial arts are inseparable. The needs of the mind and the needs of the body must both be met for human beings to truly actualize their potential.

Shortly after my graduation from USC, I decided that I wanted to teach hwa rang do rather than attend law school. Having seen what hwa rang do could do for people (and experiencing its benefits firsthand), I felt my father's love of the art burn unquenchably in my own heart and soul. This decision deeply disappointed my father, who wanted a better life for his children through higher learning. His disappointment weighed heavily on me during those years, and our relationship became distant.

In the spring of 1994, I came across an old taekwondo school that was up for lease. With a small loan, I leased the run-down space and immediately went to work renovating it. With the help of one of my first students from my first dojang of two decades before, we tore down walls, ripped up decayed flooring, and built a beautiful training hall with traditional Korean décor and modern amenities. Two years later and with a student body of more than 250 people, we had our grand opening. It was a great success. It was at this point that my father accepted my decision to teach and follow in his footsteps. His acceptance blew away the last traces of the cloud that had haunted my heart for years, and it cemented our relationship once again.

A teacher affects eternity; he can never tell where his influence stops.
                                                                    Henry B. Adams

CHAPTER 3

HWA RANG DO

INTRODUCTION

To understand the meaning of the words "hwa rang do," one must first have some basic knowledge of the history of the language of the Far East. In ancient times, China, Korea and Japan all used Chinese characters. Each region had different pronunciations of the characters and occasionally contributed local variations to their meaning. The meaning of some of these characters also changed as the language evolved with culture, art, philosophy and technology. To Koreans of the modern era, Chinese writing is seen in somewhat the same context as modern Americans view Latin; it is a language of the educated class of antiquity and a tremendous source of culture.

ETYMOLOGY OF HWA RANG DO

"Hwa" means "flower," and "rang" means "man," "groom" or "nobleman." Does that mean the Hwarang were flower men, like florists? Of course not. A flower is symbolic of many things, and its meaning depends on culture and ideology. Additionally, there are different levels of interpretation—subconscious, conscious and cosmic. To understand who the Hwarang were, we must first understand the context in which the ancient Sillans used the term.

During the Sillan era, Buddhism was the state religion, therefore we can conjecture that "hwa" represented the ideas of blossoming, enlightenment and nirvana. The ancient Hwarang were spiritual leaders in their communities, and some historians believe that local villagers thought of them as *bodhisattvas*—enlightened human beings who postponed nirvana to help other humans achieve enlightenment themselves. Because the "rang" character symbolizes a man, groom or nobleman, "hwarang" could have meant "enlightened nobleman."

Let us examine the symbolism of the flower more deeply. A flower is the essence of beauty. One cannot distinguish what single element of the flower makes it beautiful, it just is. It requires neither pretense nor effort in being beautiful. It is beautiful by its mere existence. These are qualities that the modern hwa rang do stylist aspires to emulate: being strong without trying to be strong, being kind and generous without trying to be kind and generous, loving without trying to be loving, being wise without trying to be wise. When one has to *try* to be something, he is trying to be something that he is not, or he is expressing something that he does not possess or understand. One should search within himself for these qualities and, once found, attempt to understand and exercise them until they become fully actualized.

The character for "do" in both Korean and Japanese is the symbol for a path or road. It represents the journey of life, often filled with many trials, challenges and hardships. Taoism, one of the intrinsic components of Hwarang philosophy and science, is also represented and symbolized by this character.

In the modern era, the invention of gunpowder and firearms made most hand-to-hand combat skills unnecessary in warfare, and the "do" suffix came to be used to label certain bodies of ancient martial knowledge preserved by Koreans and the Japanese. Therefore, the "do" in hwa rang do is the essential element that makes the path of the Hwarang relevant in the modern world—a way to live one's life through the exercise of martial training.

Hwa rang do is based on the ancient theory of equal opposites that interact with each other to form all things in the cosmos, as described in the *I Ching* (the "book of changes"). This concept is symbolized by yin-yang in Chinese and um-yang in Korean. It is the understanding that there is always more than one way, and for every one thing, there is an equal opposite. Practitioners of this philosophy must obtain balance and ultimately gain harmony with the natural laws and ways of the cosmos—embracing all things, as each individual is a microcosm of the universe. One must embrace death before he can truly live, one must embrace heartache before he can truly love, and one must embrace fear before he can live courageously.

This duality also lies within the name of hwa rang do itself. "Hwa," as a flower, symbolizes um (soft, delicate and feminine), whereas "rang" symbolizes yang (hard, forceful and masculine). The essence of hwa rang do is balance and harmony through understanding all possibilities and then harmonizing those possibilities into the reality of everyday living.

However, for us to arrive at this state of higher consciousness, we must journey and walk the path of life, with all its difficulties. In daily life, the pursuit of higher consciousness requires learning the consequences of your shortcomings, finding ways to overcome them, and appreciating those shortcomings as a part of your whole being. In martial applications, the path to higher consciousness requires first learning the consequences of the physical attack, learning to strengthen oneself to defend against it, and finally realizing that you can defend yourself without ever raising a hand.

THE WAY: THE STRENGTH OF THE WARRIOR'S PATH

The warrior's path is lined with the concepts of moral rectitude, self-governance, universal truth, conscience, self-awareness, honor and righteousness. These ideals and many more are essential to understanding "the way." This is the path a warrior must travel to become a hwa rang do practitioner, and it is not for everyone. Many of us lose our way and become fixated on the immediate, trite, visible material world and lose sight of why we started the journey in the first place.

Most of us have experienced this early in life. Often, during our college years, we want to make a difference in the world and accomplish something great to enhance humanity. Then life catches up to us, and we become stuck in our routines, living from one paycheck to another, always trying to make a little more money so we can enjoy a little more vacation, a little more freedom. We become stressed and pressured by life as we marry, have children, gain more responsibilities, and we begin to lose sight of our "why"—the purpose that drove us to do great things in our youth.

That is the way for us. It is not an easy path, a road paved in gold, but a path of hardship, self-doubt, harsh criticism, trials and tribulation. In order to persist on this path, one must develop strength of mind, body and spirit—the strength of a warrior. Strength does not mean the absence of weakness, nor does courage mean the absence of fear. True strength comes from those in the most vulnerable and weak situations in life, and true courage comes to those in the direst of circumstances. The value of all things comes from how much sacrifice was made to attain them. One must constantly choose to adhere to or veer from his chosen path, not based on whether a given action or path is easy but whether it is true and righteous.

As we practice the techniques to injure, maim and even kill, we more clearly understand the fragility of life and gain a renewed appreciation for it. This duality—understanding peace through violence—is a vital part of hwa rang do and is important in our daily practice; we must know the consequences of a technique and the pain it causes in order to appreciate its value. These concepts of duality are often difficult for the Western mind to accept. The occidental worldview is founded on the idea of absolutes and strives to make everything completely "good." For us, the Hwarang, a full existence and a life of strength is based on knowing and understanding all aspects of ourselves—the good and the bad, the beautiful and the ugly, the strong and the weak—while always striving for what is honorable and right, not by hiding or denying our weaknesses but by confronting and overcoming them. This is the warrior's path.

As warriors, we must live our lives every day by embracing death and, in the same way, endeavor to succeed by embracing the possibility of failure. As warriors, we must seek to do what is right for the sake of righteousness, not for the reward. This brings a profound appreciation for the value of our lives.

NEW CATEGORIZATION OF MARTIAL ARTS

Based on these principles of the warrior's path, I propose a new categorization and definition for the term "martial art" and its related terms:

Martial Sport—Learning fighting skills primarily for competitive purposes and/or fitness.

Self-Defense—Learning fighting skills primarily for practical self-defense purposes and/or fitness.

Martial Art—Learning fighting skills for competition and self-defense with the emphasis on discipline, hierarchy and tradition.

Martial Way—Learning fighting skills, understanding the strengths and weaknesses of one's self in order to build and strengthen one's character, living in accordance with the warrior's path as a way of life. It is in this martial way that hwa rang do is found.

THREE ELEMENTS OF THE SELF

In order to improve ourselves, we must understand what the self consists of. We are not just collections of muscle, skin and bones. We consist of essentially three elements that compose our entire being: the mental, physical and emotional. Like an equilateral triangle, all three elements are equally dependent on each other to create a stable structure. When the sides are balanced, a perfect circle can form within.

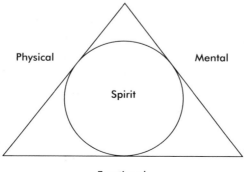

Everything in our lives is processed by these three aspects of the self. Each is equally important, and each affects the other two. For example, the process of eating lunch first starts with the physical craving of the body. The decision of what to eat often has emotional attachment, as the phrase "what do you feel like eating" indicates. The mental process might involve deciding whether we can afford our chosen dish, whether it's healthy, etc.

By understanding and being aware of these elements, we can better control our responses to external forces and maximize our human potential—the ultimate goal of hwa rang do. By developing a clear, focused mind, a strong, healthy body and a stable emotional center, we strengthen the fourth essential element, the spirit.

SPHERES OF KNOWLEDGE

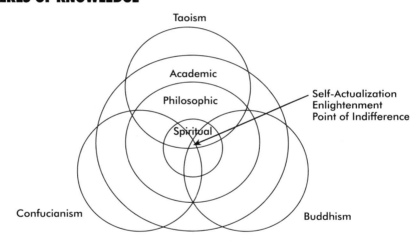

In hwa rang do, the worldview is consistent with our theory of um-yang. We believe that, if all things, ideas, energies and people were different roads, they would all converge at one "point of indifference," where all things are equal and harmonious.

A similar concept is illustrated in the above diagram. Confucianism, Taoism and Buddhism are used only as examples; the "three spheres of knowledge" can be replaced with any philosophy or worldview, and the number of spheres is infinite. A Hwarang is a seeker of truth and must study all forms of life's teachings. After acquiring a certain level of intellectual maturity and worldly experience, one begins to see universal patterns that unify all forms of knowledge and experience. With this foundation, one can start the journey toward truth.

All knowledge is first acquired by a teacher or by circumstance and is filed away in our minds for later examination. We then use logic to verify the knowledge but eventually realize that critical examination cannot validate any truth. After this epistemological journey, we finally conclude that the truth is intertwined with what is visible and invisible, finite and infinite, abstract and material; the absolute truth—the spirit—is the quintessential element that bridges these oppositions and contradictions.

CURRICULUM IN FOUR DIVISIONS

In keeping with its philosophy of maintaining balance and harmony, hwa rang do is not only an art based on self-defense. It also incorporates the Eastern healing arts, making it a truly complete system.

Dr. Joo Bang Lee divided hwa rang do's curriculum into four categories of *mu sul* (martial skills):

1. *Nae Gong*: internal power
2. *Oe Gong*: external power
3. *Mu Gi Gong*: weapon power
4. *Shin Gong*: supernatural power

Within these four divisions are more than 4,000 physical techniques, which can be further subdivided into 280 different categories.

Joo Bang Lee also divided the *in sul* (healing skills) portion of hwa rang do's curriculum into six categories:

1. *Chiapsul*: acupressure
2. *Ch'imgusul*: acupuncture and moxibustion
3. *Yakbangbop*: herbal medicine
4. *Chopgolsul*: bone setting
5. *Hwalbop*: special first-aid resuscitation techniques
6. *Kiryoksul*: healing through the use of internal energy

For the purposes of this book, we will examine the martial skills of hwa rang do.

NAE GONG

Nae gong centers on the development of one's ki power and how to control and direct it through both passive (um) and active (yang) methods. Ki power development is taught by specialized breathing and meditation exercises in conjunction with physical exercises.

The practitioner learns to develop, harness and apply this human energy resource, directing it at will to different parts of the human anatomy for different results. At more advanced levels, this power can be controlled and extended from one individual to another for both healing and combat applications. Ki is found in all living creatures, yet in the disciplined study of hwa rang do, one can learn to develop it and perform amazing physical feats, replacing previously conceived limitations with unlimited possibilities.

There are five different senses of ki, each of which can be developed by a specific hwa rang do exercise:

1. *Kyong Ki*: making the body light
2. *Chung Ki*: making the body heavy
3. *Ch'yol Ki*: making the body hard as steel
4. *Ma Ki*: making the body numb
5. *Shin Ki*: increasing mental concentration and awareness

OE GONG

Oe gong is the externalization of nae gong and takes its form in more than 4,000 offensive and defensive combat applications. Almost all martial arts systems are divided into either hard/linear or soft/circular movements, but hwa rang do combines both elements to form a combat system in harmony with the laws of nature. Most techniques are designed so that a physically weaker individual can perform them successfully on a stronger opponent, and anyone from a 3-year-old to an 80-year-old can learn them.

Oe gong instruction includes the following:

1. Hand strikes and blocks in both circular and linear motions (trapping and grabbing as well as deflection applications using the hands, the fingers, wrists, forearms, elbows, arms and shoulders), applied in both vibrating strikes and thrusting strikes.

2. Three hundred sixty-five individual kicking techniques, including linear kicks, circular kicks, snapping kicks, thrusting kicks, low kicks, aerial kicks, double-leg kicks, combination kicks, multiple kicks, and kicks from sitting and prone positions.

3. Throws and takedowns as well as acrobatics and falling techniques from any position onto any surface.

4. Human anatomical structure/function as it pertains to combat applications (for example, knowing and using the body's weak points to effectively control the opponent, regardless of his size).

5. Joint manipulation and bone breaking, pressure-point applications, containment, control and prisoner transport techniques.

6. Grappling applications (*kot'ugi*), ground fighting and submission locks.

7. Forms for each sash ranking, possessing a harmonious combination of both soft/circular with hard/linear.

8. Offensive/defensive choking and neck manipulation techniques.

9. Defense against multiple assailants.

10. Counteroffense and defense for the above and additional advanced, secret techniques.

These applications are taught as a form of combat yet with full control in order to minimize danger to the student. By practicing these diverse techniques, one can maintain or regain health through physical exercise while learning to control any attacker with minimum movement. Hwa rang do techniques are implemented to the degree a particular situation dictates, applying a precise degree of response for each incremental escalation of force.

MU GI GONG

Mu gi gong is weapons training. More than 108 different weapons are found in hwa rang do, and these weapons are divided into 20 different categories:

1. Cutting
2. Slicing
3. Chopping
4. Stabbing
5. Throwing
6. Striking
7. Grappling
8. Shooting
9. Blowing
10. Hammering
11. Sticks
12. Sectioned
13. Linked
14. Fans
15. Canes
16. Ball-shaped or round
17. Spears
18. Pin or needle weapons
19. Slings
20. Disks

Weapon techniques were traditionally kept secret lest the enemy would recognize the strategy of attack as soon as he saw the hwa rang do practitioner draw his weapon. For this reason, weapon practice outside of group military drills was always done in private, and instruction was given only to the most trusted and loyal disciples. By studying the 20 different types of weapons, it is possible to extend that knowledge and master all 108.

At the West Coast headquarters, we train essentially in the three weapons that best represent both the old and modern eras. The *changbong* (long staff), *ssangjyolbong* (two sticks connected by rope—also known as *nunchaku*) and the *changgom* (sword). After the student has mastered these three, we add a variety of weapons and practice fighting with them, using *kumdo* (Korean fencing) armor and tactics.

SHIN GONG

"Shin gong" literally means "supernatural skills." It is, at its most basic level, the study, development and control of the human mind. In order to attain one's full potential as a human being, physical strength must be augmented by mental ability, therefore techniques are taught to increase one's total awareness, focus and concentration. The truly dedicated practitioner is able to perform feats of "mind over matter" and has extraordinary healing powers, as shin gong overlaps in sul's healing methods.

Shin gong includes instruction in the following:

1. *Tok-Shim Sul*: the power to read one's thoughts or intentions

2. *Shin-Kyon Sul*: a form of telepathy

3. In Sul: the skills of extraordinary patience and tolerance

4. *Ch'oe-Myon Sul*: hypnotism

5. *Un-Shin Bop*: the art of concealment, employing a combination of distraction, suggestion, stealth and camouflage.

6. *Sa-Sang Bop*: the study of human constitutional types. Human personalities and psychological characters are broken up into four basic types—two types of um and two types of yang.

7. *Kukup Hwal-Bop*: emergency resuscitation to revive an unconscious person.

8. *Ch'imgu Sul*: the use of acupuncture and moxibustion to cure illnesses

9. *Jyopkol Sul*: the study of setting broken bones and dislocated joints

10. *Ju Sul*: the practice of chanting as a technique to heal or cause sickness

11. *Son Hak*: the study of life preservation skills, aimed at achieving immortality through the practice of Zen Buddhist meditation, wilderness survival skills, eating only natural foods, and hermitage. The capacity to

live alone for long periods of time is a highly evolved art, and it is essential for the continued study of the infinite powers of the mind.

12. *T'ae-Guk Um-Yang O-Haeng Bop*: the study of the laws of the universe based on t'ae-guk (tai chi), um-yang, and *o-haeng*'s theory of the five elements (wood, metal, fire, water and earth).

13. *Yu-Shim Bop*: the study of human emotions and thought.

These powers and more lie within every human being and can be developed and used through the proper training methods.

CHAPTER 4

UM-YANG THEORY

Um-yang is the Korean word for the Chinese yin-yang theory of Eastern metaphysics. It states that there exists an equal and opposite polar dichotomy that coexists to form everything within nature. Ancient scholars believed that ki existed long before anything else.

"In the beginning, there was only vital energy, ki, consisting of um and yang. These opposing forces moved and circulated ... As this movement gained speed, a mass of sediment was pushed together and, since there was no outlet for this, it consolidated to form the earth in the center of the universe."

Dr. Joo Bang Lee

The interaction of these two forces created all things and all life. The um-yang is symbolized by a circle with an "S"-shaped line through the middle, separating both halves equally. It is said that the symbol of um-yang is a representation of two dragons (or a dragon and phoenix) swallowing or chasing each other in constant rotation, never ending and without any beginning.

It is important to understand that the symbol is not just a circle divided into two halves; they interact to form different degrees of um and yang but create a balanced whole in summation. In order for one to exist, there must also exist its opposite: light and dark, heaven and earth, right and wrong, love and hate, good and evil, strong and weak, microcosm and macrocosm, etc. Hwa rang do's entire curriculum is based on the um-yang theory of maintaining harmony with the natural laws of the universe.

THREE ELEMENTS OF UM

1. *Yu*: the concept of soft, unrelenting motion, like flowing water. Water is soft, yet it can erode rocks and the strongest metals. Water moves in perpetual motion, unrelenting and constantly seeking the path of least resistance. It rounds angular edges and maximizes its kinetic energy. Also, water is flexible and adaptive to its environment, like when it takes the shape of its container.

2. *Won*: the concept of circular patterns. All things in life follow a cyclical pattern, starting and finishing at the same point. With circular movement, energy can be curved or redirected with minimal force while maximizing impact. Won also refers to centrifugal force—the power generated by spinning.

3. *Hap*: the concept of combining or gathering. In order to create something, one must know all of its fundamental parts before combining them to form different combinations and techniques. In these combinations and techniques, one must always maintain the concepts of efficiency and maximize energy with minimal force.

THREE ELEMENTS OF YANG

1. *Kang*: the concept of hardness, like rock or steel. Without a strong foundation, there is no stability, form or longevity. Kang also refers to the determination of the will—never giving in or yielding and always staying focused on the task at hand.

2. *Kak*: the concept of angles. All things possess shapes and patterns that create specific results or serve a particular function. Knowledge of angles enhances the understanding of form, movement and positioning in order to maximize balance and power. Kak also refers to the angles of attack and body position in relation to one's opponent and environment, with the emphasis placed on developing better orientation of attack and defense. This is particularly important in executing effective joint-manipulation techniques; with the slightest change of angle, a person's joint can

be dislocated with minimal force.

3. *Kan*: the concept of distance. One must understand the proper range of the opponent's (and his own) arms, legs or weapon in order to effectively create a defensive perimeter, as well as execute proper attacks. Proper footwork and body positioning must be practiced in order to maximize the mobility to attack and escape.

PART II – COMBAT CONCEPTS

CHAPTER 5

STAGES OF FIGHTING

There are three stages of fighting that determine different tactical and strategic responses. While some martial arts specialize in a particular stage or range, hwa rang do covers all three stages of fighting with the addition of an alternate stage—the one-knee position, or OKP.

STAGE I: *KAN'GYOK* (STAND-UP WITH DISTANCE)

This stage begins with both you and your opponent standing just outside of striking range. Kicks and punches can be landed effectively with only a slight forward movement. The primary objective in Stage I is learning to close the distance and use striking and blocking techniques with both hands and feet.

STAGE II: *CHOPHAP* (CLOSE STAND-UP)

In Stage II, both you and your opponent are in a standing clinch. The primary objectives in this range are joint manipulation, pressure points, takedowns, throws and close-range techniques such as elbows, knees and head butts. This stage begins on the feet but ends with your opponent on the ground in a nondominant position.

STAGE IIIA: *CHASE* (ONE-KNEE POSITION)

This is an alternate stage in which you are on one knee while your opponent is prone. The goal here is to finish the fight with a joint lock or submission without having to roll around on the ground in a wrestling match. Another key element in securing a victory is learning how to follow up with a submission in the prone position if the integrity of the OKP is compromised.

This stage is vital in street survival, law-enforcement and military applications in which being in a prone position decreases one's ability to defend and counter against multiple threats, while increasing the risk of losing one's sidearm.

STAGE IIIB: *TONGGYOL* (ON THE GROUND)

In this final stage, both you and your opponent are prone on the ground. Learning grappling and submission techniques is vital for success in this, the last and least favorable position in which to submit or finish your opponent.

CONCEPTS OF JOINT MANIPULATION

TYPES OF JOINT MANIPULATION

In order to effectively apply joint manipulations or joint locks, one must have a basic understanding of human anatomy. Some joints, such as elbows and knees, are hinged joints, which function in the same way a door opens and closes. Other joints, such as shoulders and hips, are ball-and-socket joints, which allow greater range of motion. All joints are laced with tendons, ligaments and muscles; tendons connect muscles to bones, and ligaments connect bones to other bones.

Joint manipulation involves placing the opponent's joint at the proper angle and applying enough pressure to deliver intense pain, dislocate the joint or break the limb. This is done to control or submit one's opponent. In this book, we will focus our attention on how to control the joints of the upper limbs, subduing the attacker with speed and precision.

AGAINST THE JOINT

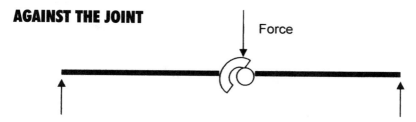

This is most effective against hinged joints—joints that only bend in one direction and do not rotate. By applying pressure directly on the joint while keeping the two connecting bones stationary, or moving them in opposite directions, the joint can be easily dislocated or hyperextended, leaving the limb useless.

ANGLED LEVERAGE

The angled leverage application is most effective when applied to ball-and-socket joints, or joints that function in a similar manner, such as the wrist, shoulder, ankle and hip. By placing the joint at a particular angle, the ligaments and tendons are extended and lose their ability to preserve the

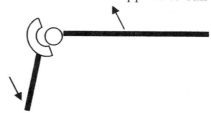

integrity of the joint. At this point, pressure can be applied to painfully force the dislocation of the ball from the socket.

TWIST AND ROTATION

The twist-and-rotation technique can be applied against both hinged and ball-and-socket joints. However, since it requires a strong grip on both sides of the joint, the twist and rotation is most effective when applied to smaller joints, such as the fingers, the wrist and sometimes the elbow. This is generally not a dislocation technique, and it is most often used as a transition to a stronger hold.

COMPRESSION

This is often called "joint sepa-ration." Compression techniques operate with the same principle as a nutcracker. By placing some-thing in the crook of the joint and applying pressure to the bones on both sides, the joint can be sepa-rated. This is most effective when applied to the elbow or knee.

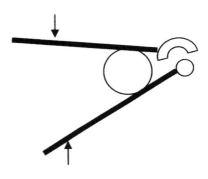

OTHER JOINT-MANIPULATION CONCEPTS

FLUIDITY

Arts such as jujutsu, judo, aikido and hapkido rely on the principle of fluid motion. Joint-manipulation techniques cannot be applied effectively with mere pushing and pulling. It is best to practice them with slow, smooth, constant movement rather than with a series of jerky, stop-and-go steps. Step-by-step practice should only be done while introducing the techniques to students so they develop basic memory patterns. As you become more adept, you should practice each technique with greater speed.

Whenever you pause during a technique, you present an opportunity for your opponent to counter. By constantly moving and keeping in con-tact with your opponent, you maintain control and dictate what he does. This is also true in life; once we attain a position of control, we must learn to capitalize and take advantage of our momentum. If an opportunity is missed, who knows when it will return? The time to rest is not when you are progressing or in the middle of a task. You must be relentless until the point of completion.

CONTROL

It is easier to control what is near than what is far. This is a simple but often overlooked idea. You must engage your opponent and move close to the point of attack. When your limbs are extended fully, the extremities possess minimum leverage and power, but by folding the arms and bringing them closer to the center of your body, you gain greater leverage from your body weight.

CHANGE THE WORLD BY CHANGING YOURSELF

It is much easier to move yourself in relation to your opponent than to move your opponent. You must control yourself before you can control others. This may seem like common sense, but as the old saying goes, common sense is not so common. You'd be surprised how many people try to muscle their opponents around rather than simply shift their own positions.

By the same token, you must understand that we control reality by controlling our perspective of the world. The world will exist whether we see it one way or another. Whether this is an ultimate truth or not, it helps to understand as a martial artist that you are the one in power and that you can control outcomes by controlling yourself.

This idea is essential when executing techniques for combat. If you want your opponent closer to you, then you move closer to your opponent. If you want him to be by your side, then you move to his side. For instance, in executing a takedown, lifting a person and throwing him like a sack of potatoes is very difficult and unrealistic. Instead, you should lower your body to the ground and take your opponent down with you. Putting yourself in the position of greatest advantage in relation to your opponent should be your primary goal. This concept applies to stand-up fighting, to ground fighting and to life.

USE REVERSE PSYCHOLOGY

It is natural for your opponent to always do the opposite of what you want him to do. If you pull, he will probably resist and pull back. If you push, he will push back. Therefore, you should be mindful of his responses and set him up to gain the advantage. The best way to control a person is to allow him to think it was his decision to move to a certain position.

VIBRATION VERSUS CONSTANT PRESSURE

There are different kinds of impacting blows, and vibrating pressure is the most effective for dislocating joints. Vibrating pressure is like a bull-whip. It is achieved by rapidly tensing your muscles to create a sudden forward thrust, then immediately relaxing and retracting the pressure. Constant pressure, on the other hand, is used to control your opponent by his joints, without dislocation. Your muscles are held in a state of contraction to apply steady force on the limb.

PHYSICAL KI

While applying any technique, make sure to tighten the lower abdomen, which is the center of ki power. Regardless of whether you believe in the existence of physical ki, tightening your abdomen will keep your back and center aligned while engaging your core muscles, thus allowing you to deliver greater force with any movement.

MENTAL KI

Mental ki is energy created by strong concentration of your mind and will, and it is just as important and powerful as physical ki. You must maintain focus and intent on the task at hand and allow nothing to divert your attention.

HANDS: YOUR PRIMARY WEAPONS

A craftsman should know every aspect of his tools, and a martial artist should consider his body a tool for self-defense. Your hands are your primary weapons, and in order to maximize their use, you must understand their function.

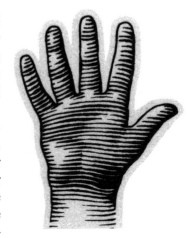

Note, for instance, that the last three fingers of your hand are mainly for gripping, whereas the index finger and thumb are for dexterity. As you can see by observing your hand, most of the muscles are below the pinkie finger and the thumb. These areas are known as the thenar and hypothenar eminences. The only function of muscle is to contract, and because the index finger lies the farthest from the hand's dense musculature, it is virtually useless for gripping.

Pointing the index finger directs the release of ki power and creates what we call ki extension. This is why we use the index finger naturally when we point at objects, people, or while giving directions. We should also use this concept when we grip our opponent. By extending the index finger, the hand gains greater agility by not engaging the muscles of the forearm, and the index finger guides the direction of applied force.

STEPPING

While there are many ways to use footwork, the most basic and effective patterns involve moving to the inside or outside of the opponent.

INSIDE POSITION

Moving to the inside of your opponent makes the front of his body vulnerable to attack, but it also creates the opportunity for him to counter.

OUTSIDE POSITION

This is a more advantageous position. The only way for the opponent to counter from this position is to turn around (with a spinning back kick, for example). Here, the available target areas are found behind the opponent, such as the base of his skull, the kidney, the back of the knee, etc.

TYPES OF GRIPS AND ARM CONTROL

The success of any joint-manipulation technique depends on the proper grip. The following are used in hwa rang do to place the joints at the proper angles.

TWO-HAND THUMBS-CROSSED GRIP

The opponent's hand (left) is controlled by both of your hands, and crossing your thumbs adds greater strength to the grip. The thumbs can then push against the back of the opponent's hand to secure the proper wrist angle and torque.

HAND-AND-WRIST GRIP

It is important to have a tight grip around the opponent's wrist and hand, with all of the opponent's fingers trapped (the thumb can be left outside the grip without compromising its integrity).

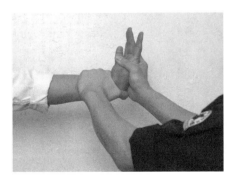

HAND-AND-ELBOW GRIP

Here, the opponent's hand is controlled by the thumb. This gives you control over the direction of the hand and makes it difficult for your opponent to escape the grip.

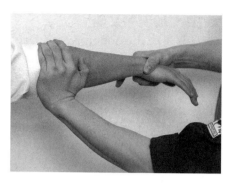

UNDERARM GRIP

This position is a transitional hold that can move into a hand grip. Often, it is difficult to attain control of an opponent's hand or wrist, and much easier to instead trap it under your arm. This is also a good position to defend against armed attacks. Notice the use of the other hand to secure the elbow.

INSIDE UNDERARM

With the opponent's thumb pointing inward.

OUTSIDE UNDERARM

With the opponent's thumb pointing outward.

OVER-SHOULDER GRIP

This, like the underarm grip, also works as a transitional hold. The over-shoulder grip is used when the opponent's limb rests higher on your body. It brings you closer to a clinching position by advancing your control up the opponent's arm to his elbow, and it is best used when his hand is too difficult to grab or when he is retracting his arm. To prevent your opponent from flexing his arm and attempting a head lock, your hands should be around the elbow and forearm.

INSIDE OVER-SHOULDER

With the opponent's thumb pointing inward.

OVER-SHOULDER

With the opponent's thumb pointing outward.

FIGURE-FOUR GRIP

The figure-four grip is one of the most effective and powerful holds. It provides excellent leverage because both hands attack the opponent's one arm.

INSIDE FIGURE-FOUR

From the inside position with the opponent's thumb pointing inward.

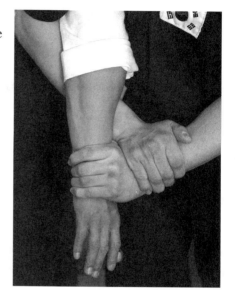

OUTSIDE FIGURE-FOUR

From the outside position with the opponent's thumb pointing outward.

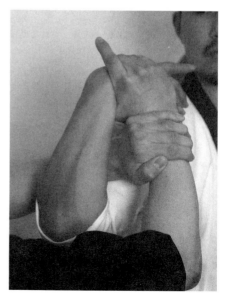

CATCHING THE ARM

Before applying any grip, you must gain control of your opponent's limb. The following are ways to block and catch the arm. (For the sake of consistency, each attack will be made with the right arm.)

TOP BLOCK CATCHES

Using the common upper or "top" block, you can acquire the two-hand thumbs-crossed grip or underarm grip.

TWO-HAND THUMBS-CROSSED GRIP

INSIDE CATCH

Block from the inside position with the left hand, swing your opponent's arm downward and counterclockwise into your right hand, and acquire the two-hand thumbs-crossed grip (see page 66).

OUTSIDE CATCH

Block from the outside position with the right hand and swing the arm downward and clockwise into your left hand, acquiring the grip.

UNDERARM GRIP

INSIDE CATCH

After executing a top block from inside with the left hand, circle counterclockwise over your opponent's arm and trap his forearm in your left armpit. Use the other hand to control his elbow for added security.

OUTSIDE CATCH

After executing a top block from the outside position with the right hand, circle clockwise over your opponent's arm and trap it in your right armpit. Remember to control the elbow with your free hand.

DOWN BLOCK CATCHES

These techniques first use a downward block to deflect a low attack, then transition to a hand-and-wrist or over-shoulder grip. Note that the opponent's arm must be swung around and brought up to a higher position before administering the hold.

HAND-AND-WRIST GRIP

INSIDE CATCH

Block downward with the left hand, swing your opponent's arm clockwise and catch his hand in your right hand, next to your face, while grabbing his wrist with your left hand.

OUTSIDE CATCH

Block downward with the right hand, swing the arm counterclockwise and catch his hand with your left hand while grabbing his wrist with your right hand.

OVER-SHOULDER GRIP

INSIDE CATCH

Follow the low block and loop your left arm clockwise around and over the opponent's elbow, bringing his forearm to rest on top of your left shoulder. Use your shoulder to trap your opponent's forearm while your hands establish better control over the limb.

OUTSIDE CATCH

Blocking with the right hand, follow the bloc k and loop your arm counterclockwise around and over the opponent's elbow, bringing his forearm to rest on top of your right shoulder. Be sure to control the arm with both hands.

CROSS-TOP BLOCK CATCH

This catch is very strong and effective, but it leaves you somewhat unprotected because both arms are raised in order to deal with the opponent's strike. Note that your wrists are crossed, and both hands close like a pair of scissors to acquire the hand-and-elbow grip.

HAND-AND-ELBOW GRIP

INSIDE CATCH

Block the strike, then step to the inside position (see page 65). Push the arm down with your left hand while grabbing the wrist, clearing the way for your right hand to grab the elbow.

OUTSIDE CATCH

Block the strike, then step to the outside position (see page 65). Push the arm down with your right hand while grabbing the wrist, clearing the way for your left hand to grab the elbow.

CROSS-DOWN BLOCK CATCH

Like the cross-top block catch, this technique also leaves you somewhat unprotected, as both arms are momentarily lowered to block the strike, but it provides an excellent transition to the hand-and-wrist grip.

HAND-AND-WRIST GRIP

INSIDE CATCH

Block the arm and step to the inside position. From the cross block, grab the thumb side of your opponent's hand with your left hand and swing it around counterclockwise in front of you, placing your right hand on the wrist for added control.

HAND-AND-WRIST GRIP

OUTSIDE CATCH

Catch the arm and step to the outside position. From the cross block, grab the pinkie-finger side of your opponent's hand with your right hand and swing it around clockwise in front of you, placing your left hand on the wrist for added control.

INSIDE/OUTSIDE SOFT BLOCK CATCH

For this catch, both hands are used in conjunction—one follows the pathway of the other in a clockwise or counterclockwise orbit. One advantage to this is that, if one hand misses, you still have the other hand to rely on. The hands must be relaxed and used like a whip to wrap around the opponent's arms.

INSIDE CATCH

Block the opponent's punch with your right palm and grab the wrist while looping your left hand counterclockwise around the opponent's forearm, securing a tight hold.

OUTSIDE CATCH

Block the punch with your left palm and grab the wrist while looping your right hand clockwise around the forearm, securing the hold.

OUTSIDE/INSIDE SOFT BLOCK CATCH

Because the opponent's arm is being pushed in one direction, this technique can be used to throw him off-balance.

INSIDE CATCH

Block the strike at the wrist with your left hand, turn the arm counterclockwise and immediately grab the inside of the elbow with your right hand.

OUTSIDE CATCH

Block the strike at the wrist with your right hand, turn the arm clockwise and immediately grab the outside of the elbow with your left hand.

GROUND CONTROL

TWO TYPES OF GROUND CONTROL

In hwa rang do, we believe in maintaining control of the opponent throughout the entire encounter, from stand-up fighting to ground fighting. Unlike many other grappling arts, going to the ground with your opponent is a last resort for the hwa rang do practitioner; generally, it is more prudent to remain on your feet or in the OKP, which is used often in hwa rang do techniques.

In most practical applications of self-defense, law-enforcement and military training, ground fighting should never be the primary goal, because one never knows whether others are waiting to attack with their bare hands or with weapons. Though there are ways to defend yourself and maintain a safe perimeter while on the ground, it is not a favorable option.

SUBMISSION (FINISHING HOLD)

A submission occurs when your opponent is placed in a hold from which he cannot escape, and he must submit (usually by "tapping out") to avoid injury and be released. Submission holds include chokes, armbars, neck cranks and joint manipulations. Usually, both you and your opponent are on the ground when a submission is used.

QUICK LOCK (TEMPORARY HOLD)

A quick lock is performed from the OKP to temporarily immobilize your opponent with a joint lock, neck crank, choke, or by using pressure points. It generally serves as a transition to finish the opponent with another submission or a strike, but often this position is enough to control him and end the fight. If the quick lock is compromised, however, it can serve as an excellent transition to go to the ground and submit the opponent from there.

ESCAPING OR COUNTERING JOINT LOCKS

The principle of "following the path of least resistance" applies here. Resisting and going against a joint lock will add more pressure to the joint, causing greater pain and possibly a dislocation. To escape or counter a joint lock, one must move in the direction of the pressure being applied, not against it. This contradicts our normal response to pain—we reflexively move in opposition to the source of the discomfort, trying to escape it, but we must train ourselves to move into the technique and not away.

Following the path of least resistance might be an ideal principle in the application of physical techniques, but it is not applicable to the moral philosophy of Hwarang. For a guide to living one's life, we must choose another phrase that is more viable for a warrior: "Following the path of least resistance is what makes rivers and men crooked."

PART III – HWA RANG DO IN ACTION

CHAPTER 6

THE TECHNIQUES

INTRODUCTION

In hwa rang do, there are more than 4,000 different defenses, takedowns and submissions, and these are applicable in all types of physical attacks, all stages of fighting, and in every possible position. Because it would be impossible to cover the entire hwa rang do curriculum in one book, the focus here will be on joint-manipulation techniques. I've selected 17 of these techniques that I believe are the most widely used, and they can be acquired from Stage I all the way through Stage III with fluid transitions and without losing control of the opponent. Note that each Stage I attack—whether it is a choke, strike, lapel grab, etc.—is directed to the upper body with one or both of the opponent's arms. The joint-manipulation techniques will focus on the wrist, the elbow and the shoulder.

I've tried to vary the takedowns in Stage II and Stage III, using mostly joint-lock takedowns rather than other, weaker techniques. In Stage III, I often use the highly practical quick locks from the one-knee position (OKP) because I believe they have not been widely seen outside of hwa rang do. You'll also notice that I usually finish Stage III using the initial joint lock from Stage I, thereby keeping a sense of continuity.

If you have marginal or minimal joint-manipulation experience, you should exercise tremendous caution when practicing these techniques. It is essential that you first have them performed on you, so you learn the limitations of your own body and understand the pain and discomfort the techniques cause. When I conduct seminars, black belts from striking arts often say to me, "Wow, that really hurts. How do you know how much pressure to apply before you dislocate the joint?"

My standard answer is, "I have never dislocated a joint or broken a bone that I did not intend to. Much practice."

For beginners, I hope the following chapters stir interest in the world of joint locks. And for experienced joint-manipulators, I hope this text offers additional insights in the application and execution of these techniques.

C-LOCKS   sonmok kkokki   손목꺽기

OUTSIDE C-LOCK   oesonmok kkokki   외손목꺽기
EXPLANATION

The C-lock is one of the most widely used wrist-manipulation techniques. It is executed by obtaining a 90-degree angle on the wrist and elbow in order to form a rough "C" shape with the opponent's arm and hand. There are many ways to obtain this hold, but the most important element is to control the hand and get the proper angle on the wrist.

KEY POINTS TO ENHANCE EFFECTIVENESS
STAGE I: ACQUIRING THE GRIP AND ANGLE

In order for the C-lock to be effective, the proper angle is required. Grab the opponent's right hand with your left hand and twist outward while using your right hand to place greater pressure on the wrist. In this illustration, I'm using a right knifehand to show where to apply the pressure on my opponent's hand. However, this is not an ideal technique in a real-life situation because the knifehand could slip off in a struggle. While it is OK to secure the hold with only one hand, it is better to use both hands for the takedown. Downward pressure should be placed on the pinkie knuckle to apply maximum force, which will allow you to take your opponent to the ground.

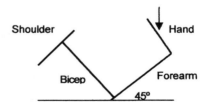

C-Lock diagram

A common mistake occurs when one pulls the wrist and inadvertently straightens the arm, thereby losing the angle and the integrity of the C-lock. If this happens, you might be able to pull your opponent to the ground by brute strength. If your opponent is larger, however, it is highly unlikely that the takedown will be successful. The following illustrations demonstrate how to acquire the C-lock against different attacks.

PUNCH

1: Instructor Jerry Kang (left) prepares to punch Master Taejoon Lee.

2: As Kang steps in with a right cross, Master Lee steps back with his right foot to maintain a safety zone. He parries the punch with his left hand and grabs Kang's wrist.

3: As the punch loses its momentum, Master Lee turns Kang's hand outward and applies an outside C-lock.

LAPEL GRAB

1: Kang grabs Master Lee's lapel with his right hand.

2: Master Lee steps back while grabbing Kang's right hand, pulling him off-balance.

3: He then slides forward while turning Kang's wrist with both hands, administering an outside C-lock. (Note that Master Lee leans his torso over the wrist for greater leverage and power, so the lock is secure regardless of whether Kang releases his grip.)

WRIST GRAB

1: Kang grabs Master Lee's right wrist with his right hand.

2: Master Lee circles his right hand counterclockwise and applies the C-lock grip with his left hand.

3: Continuing the counterclockwise motion, Master Lee frees his right wrist and uses his right palm to press on Kang's pinkie knuckle, engaging the outside C-lock.

CHOKE

1: Kang reaches forward and chokes Master Lee with both hands.

2: Master Lee steps back, drawing Kang off-balance by pulling Kang's left arm downward while gripping Kang's right hand with his left hand.

3: He then turns Kang's right wrist outward with his left hand, administering the C-lock.

REAR SHOULDER GRAB

1: With his right hand, Kang grabs Master Lee's shoulder from behind.

2: Master Lee steps out with his left foot and pivots to face Kang. He simultaneously grabs Kang's wrist with his left hand and strikes his thumb with a right knifehand to disengage the grip.

3: He continues by circling his left hand counterclockwise and applying the C-lock.

KNIFE ATTACK

1: Kang threatens Master Lee with a knife.

2: As he lunges forward, Master Lee steps back and parries with his left hand, then slides his hand up to Kang's wrist.

3: Master Lee loops Kang's wrist around counterclockwise, establishing the outside C-lock.

STAGE II: SETUP AND TAKEDOWN

Once the proper grip and angles are acquired, the takedown is easy. As is shown in the picture, step through with the leg that is on the same side as the hand that controls your opponent's pinkie knuckle (in this case, the right leg). By stepping into it, you apply all your body weight to that single point, creating extreme pressure on the wrist. Once again, the goal is to create maximum leverage, so two hands always have the advantage over only one hand.

1: Master Lee grips both sides of Kang's hand to establish total control over the wrist, and he steps through with his right leg.

2: As he drops to his left knee, Master Lee continues moving his hands counterclockwise while maintaining the angle on the wrist and arm, and Kang is cast into the air.

3: When Kang lands on his back, Master Lee pulls and straightens the arm over Kang's head.

STAGE III: GROUND LOCKUP
VARIATION 1: SHIN-ON-ELBOW QUICK LOCK

After the takedown, one can use this quick lock, which provides temporary control for finishing with either a strike or a dislocation. In this technique, I'm using an elbow hyperextension, which is a type of armbar in which my right shin drops just above the opponent's elbow while my hands pull up on his wrist and hand, breaking the arm.

1: While maintaining control over Kang's wrist, Master Lee extends Kang's arm, pinning it palm-down over his head while kneeling on the triceps tendon with his right shin.

2: As he stands up, Master Lee sharply yanks the arm upward, breaking Kang's elbow across his shin.

3: He finishes by punching Kang in the face.

IMPORTANT THINGS TO REMEMBER

1. You must maintain control of the opponent's hand in order to control the direction and position of the elbow.

2. The arm must be extended straight above the shoulders, near the head, and should not be placed perpendicular to the body, out to the side. By placing the arm to the side, the opponent has greater leverage to move his shoulders and redirect or bend his elbow, and he might squirm free.

3. Place your shin, not your knee, on the opponent's elbow. The knee is round and blunt, and the shin is much sharper. Also, the knee can easily slip off, while the shin allows for a much greater margin of error.

4. Don't kneel on the ground with both knees; be sure to place one knee down to pin or break the elbow. It is more difficult to recover to a standing position from both knees than if you're only on one, and this might be necessary if your position gets unstable and you need a quick escape. The second reason deals with the transfer of weight in your attack. If you are on both knees, your body weight is spread out equally, whereas if you drop your weight on one knee, all of your body weight is applied to the opponent's elbow.

5. You might think that your opponent can kick at you or counter, but this is difficult if you apply the proper pressure. You must make sure to push down with your knee while lifting his hand. He might be able to reach you, in which case you should block with one hand while maintaining the grip on your opponent's hand with the other. Kicks from a supine position are usually very weak, but you should still be aware of your opponent's legs.

VARIATION 2: ONE-KNEE POSITION ARMBAR

Once again, I am using the OKP. This is another quick lock, and it can transition to an armbar on the ground. It is an excellent technique because, in conjunction with the foot stomp, it neutralizes your opponent before you fully submit him.

1: Master Lee steps over Kang's arm and stomps his face with his right foot.

2: He then slips his foot underneath Kang's neck while extending his arm.

3: Master Lee finishes by pulling the arm to his chest and snapping the elbow against his thigh. (Note that Master Lee's left knee stays on the ground and his feet are far enough apart to provide a stable base.)

IMPORTANT THINGS TO REMEMBER

1. Immediately stomp the face, preferably the side of the jaw or temple which is facing you. This will inflict the most damage and cause your opponent to turn his head away from you, and you then can slip your foot under his neck, securing your leg position and preventing him from turning toward you.

2. Depending on the length of your opponent's arm, you must adjust your position and either stoop down or stand taller to make sure his elbow is against the inside of your thigh. If his elbow is under your thigh, he will have a greater chance of bending his arm, in which case you could apply a shoulder crank.

3. Make sure to press your right knee inward (as in the introductory picture) and maintain constant contact and pressure on the elbow. Make sure to also position your other leg widely enough to maintain balance in the OKP. Although your left knee is on the ground, you can kneel your right knee on his neck for additional pressure if your position is compromised.

4. To hyperextend the elbow, just bridge your hips forward and pull back on your opponent's hand.

TWO-HAND C-LOCK   yidan kkokki   이단꺽기
EXPLANATION

The two-hand C-lock is similar to the outside C-lock, but it has a modified hand position. One hand is placed on the opponent's hand, near the wrist, while the other controls the elbow. This adds more pressure to the shoulder, which can be dislocated with the proper vibrational force.

Like the outside C-lock, the two-hand C-lock requires controlling the hand and forcing the wrist and elbow into a 90-degree angle, creating a "C" shape. If the grip on the opponent's hand is compromised, you can transition into an L-lock (see Chapter 7), which places pressure on the shoulder.

KEY POINTS TO ENHANCE EFFECTIVENESS
STAGE I: ACQUIRING THE GRIP AND ANGLE

In the following examples, the right hand pushes the opponent's hand outward, while the left pulls his elbow inward. With quick vibrational force, the shoulder can be dislocated. Remember to maintain the 90-degree angle on both the wrist and elbow.

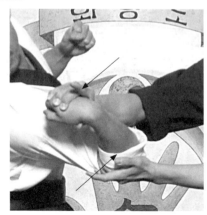

PUNCH

1: Kang prepares to punch Master Lee.

2: Master Lee deflects the punch at the wrist and elbow with an outside/inside block while stepping back.

3: As the punch loses momentum, Master Lee advances at a slight angle with his right foot while bending Kang's elbow and wrist into a two-hand C-lock.

LAPEL GRAB

1: Kang grabs Master Lee's lapel with his right hand.

2: Master Lee steps back to pull Kang off-balance while looping his right hand over Kang's hand, establishing control of the wrist. He then pulls the elbow with his left hand to prepare for the C-lock.

3: Master Lee bends Kang's wrist and elbow and administers the C-lock.

90

WRIST GRAB

1: Kang grabs Master Lee's right wrist with his right hand and prepares to strike him.

2: Master Lee makes a circular motion with his right hand and sidesteps to the left, escaping Kang's grasp. He then steps back with his right foot and applies a downward armbar.

3: As Kang tries to regain his balance by pulling backward, Master Lee follows his momentum with the C-lock.

CHOKE

1: Kang reaches forward and chokes Master Lee with both hands.

2: While stepping back with his right foot, Master Lee loops both hands clockwise, landing on the outside of Kang's right arm and wrist.

3: With a short shuffle of his left foot, he turns toward Kang and applies the C-lock, pulling the elbow with his left hand and locking the wrist outward with his right.

REAR SHOULDER GRAB

1: Kang grabs Master Lee's shoulder from behind.

2: Pivoting on his right foot, Master Lee spins around to disengage Kang's grab and control his wrist and elbow.

3: Stepping forward with his left foot, he applies the C-lock.

KNIFE ATTACK

1: Kang threatens Master Lee with an overhead reverse-grip knife attack.

2: As Kang swings, Master Lee darts to the side and parries the attack at the elbow and wrist.

3: He applies the C-lock by cranking the wrist and pulling the elbow in.

STAGE II: SETUP AND TAKEDOWN
VARIATION 1: WRIST THROW

As with the outside C-lock takedown, step through with the leg that is on the same side as the hand that controls your opponent's hand. Drop to your left knee in order to get the most out of your body weight, which will easily take the opponent to the ground. Rotating and pivoting are not the essential elements of this takedown; it is more important to use driving, constant force on the hand while pulling the elbow in the opposite direction. The most common mistake associated with this throw occurs when one swings his arms across his body, either laterally or horizontally, and tries to muscle his opponent to the ground. This is dangerous, because it increases the chance of losing the proper 90-degree angle of the wrist and elbow.

Notice also the control of the elbow. If this is lost, the C-lock will no longer work and you must transition into a different technique. However, do not panic and abandon the entire hold. As long as you maintain a grip on the hand, there are many other options.

1: While maintaining the C-lock, Master Lee kneels on his left knee to further upset Kang's balance.

2: By continuing the push-pull motion on Kang's wrist and arm, he flips Kang over.

3: Master Lee maintains control of Kang's arm after he lands.

VARIATION 2: SPINNING SHOULDER THROW

Place your right forearm underneath your opponent's right triceps, close to his armpit, to create the proper leverage. Be sure to maintain the C-lock by keeping your right hand on his hand and your left hand pulling on his elbow.

Control his elbow to ensure that it does not slip off your forearm. In the event that it does, however, this technique easily transitions back into the two-hand C-lock.

1: Master Lee firmly grips Kang's hand and elbow, preparing for the throw.

2: Master Lee raises Kang's arm over his shoulder and slides back with his left foot, placing his right hip just inside of Kang's right hip. (Note that his feet are square with Kang's.)

3: With his hip placed lower than Kang's, Master Lee throws him by straightening his legs and bending at the waist, placing extreme pressure on Kang's wrist.

STAGE III: GROUND LOCKUP
VARIATION 1: OUTSIDE KNEE-ON-NECK WRIST QUICK LOCK

This is another quick lock that can be used to immobilize your opponent or transition into a submission. If he has his chin down and is facing straight up, apply pressure with your left hand to the pressure point below his ear (or under the jaw to the lymph nodes) to force him to turn his head and expose his neck, then kneel on it.

1: After the takedown, Master Lee traps Kang's elbow in the crook of his arm while tightly flexing Kang's wrist.

2: While maintaining the wrist lock, he uses his left hand to dig into the pressure point under Kang's jaw line, forcing him to expose the side of his neck.

3: Master Lee finishes by sliding his left knee over Kang's neck and dropping his weight on it while bringing his left hand back to secure the wrist lock

IMPORTANT THINGS TO REMEMBER

1. To prevent escape, be sure to hold your opponent's elbow tightly in the crook of your arm while pressing your body forward.

2. Cup your left hand over your right to maintain greater control.

3. Do not drop to the ground with both knees, because it will not provide a stable base.

4. Bridge (push your hips forward and arch your back) or sit up to exert greater pressure on the wrist.

5. Your opponent will probably squirm and try to turn toward you, so keep his right shoulder upward and your knee on the side of his neck to prevent him from doing so. If he turns away from you, it will place greater tension on his wrist.

VARIATION 2: INSIDE KNEE-ON-NECK WRIST QUICK LOCK

This is another option once your opponent is on the ground. Place your leg over his shoulder and around his arm, stomp on the side of his face, and slip your foot under his neck.

This is a quick lock on the wrist, but it holds a very high probability of submission. Notice how the knee is forced down on the neck, creating intense pain and counterbalancing the upward pull on the wrist.

1: Master Lee steps over Kang's arm with his right foot and drops his heel on his jaw.

2: He slips his foot under Kang's neck.

3: He finishes by dropping his shin on Kang's neck while bending his wrist inward.

INSIDE CIRCLE-UNDER C-LOCK sonmok nae hoejon kkokki

손목내회전꺽기

EXPLANATION

The inside circle-under C-lock can be found in numerous martial arts and in many films. A dynamic and often misunderstood technique, it is a signature move in hwa rang do and requires some detailed examination.

KEY POINTS TO ENHANCE EFFECTIVENESS
STAGE I: ACQUIRING THE GRIP AND ANGLE

The important thing to realize is that the grip itself—the two-hand thumbs-crossed grip—is not complex. Both hands grab the opponent's hand, with the four fingers in front and the thumbs crossed over each other on the back. No special angles are applied with the grip itself. Pressure is put on the wrist only when you rotate under the opponent's arm for the takedown.

PUNCH

1: Kang prepares to strike Master Lee.

2: As Kang punches, Master Lee initiates a top block catch with his left hand and steps in at an angle with his right foot.

3: He grabs Kang's hand in a two-hand thumbs-crossed grip and swings it downward and counterclockwise.

LAPEL GRAB

1: Kang grabs Master Lee's lapel.

2: Master Lee slides back with his left foot while striking Kang's wrist with his right forearm, dislodging his grip. He simultaneously catches Kang's hand with his left hand.

3: Master Lee grabs Kang's hand with the two-hand thumbs-cross grip and swings it downward and counterclockwise.

WRIST GRAB

1: Kang grabs Master Lee's wrist and prepares to pull him into a punch.

2: Before Kang can punch, Master Lee circles his left hand counterclockwise around Kang's wrist.

3: Continuing the motion, he grips Kang's hand with the two-hand thumbs-crossed grip.

CHOKE

1: Kang chokes Master Lee with both hands.

2: Master Lee grabs Kang's right wrist with his left hand, loops his right elbow over and down on Kang's left elbow, and steps back with his left foot. He then grips Kang's right hand with his right hand.

3: Master Lee swings Kang's right wrist down and around in a counterclockwise loop.

REAR SHOULDER GRAB

1: Kang grabs Master Lee's shoulder from behind.

2: Master Lee spins around on his right foot. He knocks Kang's grip loose with a right knifehand strike to the thumb and catches Kang's hand with his left hand.

3: He applies the grip with both hands and swings his arms in a counterclockwise loop.

99

KNIFE ATTACK

1: Kang threatens Master Lee with an overhead reverse-grip knife attack.

2: Master Lee steps in with his right foot while deflecting Kang's wrist with his left hand.

3: He catches the hand with the top block catch, applies the grip, and swings Kang's wrist down counterclockwise with both hands.

STAGE II: SETUP AND TAKEDOWN

To execute the takedown after acquiring the grip, step out with your right foot, then step through with your left as you whip your opponent's arm overhead in a large counterclockwise arc. Once your left foot touches down, it is essential that you drop to your left knee to tighten the torque on his wrist. By dropping his arm, you prevent your opponent from spinning underneath and out of your lock. As long as you have the proper angle and the correct grip, it is easy to apply pressure on the pinkie knuckle with a slight twist and take your opponent to the ground and/or dislocate the wrist.

Remember not to pull the arm laterally. Push downward instead, and maintain constant pressure on the wrist. If the arm straightens and the 90-degree angle is compromised, just twist the wrist inward and toward your opponent and the angle will be easily reacquired, or use the sweeping technique explained below. Also, while spinning under the arm, avoid standing too high with your back arched and your hands behind your head, as this will weaken your balance and give your opponent the opportunity to spin out of the hold.

1: Continuing the counterclockwise motion, Master Lee steps through with his left foot, placing great stress on Kang's shoulder and elbow.

2: He pivots and kneels on his left knee, maintaining the angle on Kang's arm and increasing the torque.

3: By applying pressure to the pinkie knuckle with the heel of his palm, Master Lee throws Kang.

IF YOUR OPPONENT ATTEMPTS TO BLOCK THE THROW, USE THE FOLLOWING TECHNIQUE:

1: Stepping through with his left foot, Master Lee prepares to throw Kang.

2: Kang counters by trying to straighten his arm, and Master Lee places his right shoulder firmly against Kang's elbow.

3: Maintaining constant pressure on the elbow, Master Lee sweeps the inside of Kang's rear leg with his right foot and lowers his center of gravity, throwing Kang.

STAGE III: GROUND LOCKUP
VARIATION 1: INSIDE KNEE-ON-NECK ARMBAR

This is similar to the inside knee-on-neck wrist quick lock. It is a very tight position and works well for transitions or a quick dislocation.

1: Master Lee maintains control of Kang's wrist. He steps over Kang's arm with his right leg and stomps on his face, then slips his foot underneath Kang's neck.

2: He drops his shin sharply onto Kang's neck.

3: Master Lee pulls Kang's arm across his thigh and toward his chest. He then sits up and arches, hyperextending the elbow.

VARIATION 2: GROUND ARMBAR

The ground armbar is a popular joint lock on the ground. In hwa rang do, the ground armbar is the final option when other quick locks become unstable or otherwise compromised.

1: While maintaining control over Kang's wrist with his left hand, Master Lee hugs the elbow with his right arm.

2: Master Lee steps over Kang's head with his left foot and squeezes his arm between his inner thighs.

3: He finishes by falling back and arching while hugging Kang's arm close to his chest, hyperextending the elbow.

IMPORTANT THINGS TO REMEMBER

1. As with all armbars, be sure to apply pressure slightly above the elbow toward the shoulder, in this case with the crotch.

2. You must maintain constant contact and pressure on the opponent's elbow. Squeeze your thighs inward to prevent the elbow from moving. If he can move, he has the potential to escape.

3. Keep your feet planted firmly on the ground or pressed against the opponent's body and head for leverage. Place your leg over his head to prevent him from turning and rolling out of the hold. In a self-defense situation, however, he might try to bite your calf, so place your foot against his face. You can also stomp his face with your heel.

4. Be sure to control the opponent's wrist so he can't turn his elbow and mitigate the hyperextending force.

103

OUTSIDE REVERSE C-LOCK sonmok oe hoejon kkokki

손목외회전꺽기

EXPLANATION

The outside reverse C-lock twists the wrist inward toward the opponent's body. This hold is very effective in the application of come-along or assailant-transport techniques, as it can be easily applied in different directions.

KEY POINTS TO ENHANCE EFFECTIVENESS
STAGE I: ACQUIRING THE GRIP AND ANGLE

In this technique, the wrist is bent without using the circle-under movement. The technique will work even if the hand is closed or gripping a weapon, as shown here.

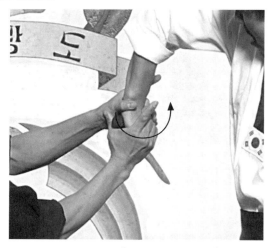

The twist-and-rotation principle applies. The left hand controls the opponent's wrist, and the right hand controls the opponent's hand and exerts most of the pressure. Both hands rotate in the same direction. The left hand must not over-rotate, however; it works more to secure the opponent's wrist and follow the right hand. If the grip is compromised, move the right hand to the two-hand thumbs-crossed grip.

PUNCH

1: Kang prepares to strike Master Lee.

2: As he punches, Master Lee steps back with his right foot, trapping Kang's punch with both hands using a modified top block catch.

3: Master Lee wrenches the wrist counterclockwise into an outside reverse C-lock and, by pivoting into Kang, lifts him to his toes.

LAPEL GRAB

1: Kang grabs Master Lee's lapel with his right hand.

2: Master Lee steps back with his right foot, pulling Kang off-balance while breaking his grip with both hands.

3: Master Lee wrenches the wrist counterclockwise into an outside reverse C-lock and pivots into Kang.

WRIST GRAB

1: Kang grabs Master Lee's right wrist with his right hand and prepares to strike him.

2: Master Lee steps back with his right foot and pulls Kang off-balance while circling his right hand under and around Kang's wrist, trapping it with his free hand.

3: Master Lee wrenches the wrist counterclockwise into an outside reverse C-lock and pivots into Kang.

CHOKE

1: Kang chokes Master Lee with both hands.

2: Stepping back and turning abruptly to the right, Master Lee dislodges Kang's grip and traps his right hand between both palms.

3: Master Lee wrenches the wrist counterclockwise into an outside reverse C-lock and pivots into Kang.

REAR SHOULDER GRAB

1: Kang grabs Master Lee's shoulder with his right hand.

2: Master Lee pivots clockwise on his right foot around the outside of Kang's arm and grabs his wrist with both hands.

3: Master Lee wrenches the wrist counterclockwise into an outside reverse C-lock and pivots into Kang.

KNIFE ATTACK

1: Kang threatens Master Lee with a knife.

2: As Kang lunges forward, Master Lee sidesteps and turns his body to the right to minimize his exposed surface area. He grabs Kang's wrist with both hands in a palm-up position.

3: By swinging his body back toward Kang, Master Lee wrenches the wrist into an outside reverse C-lock. The pain will likely cause Kang to drop the weapon.

STAGE II: SETUP AND TAKEDOWN
VARIATION 1: OUTSIDE REVERSE C-LOCK THROW

This takedown is applied by stepping under the opponent's arm with the right foot, then rotating to the left and going down to your right knee. Be sure to maintain a solid grip on the opponent's hand and create tremendous torque on his wrist. This tension, along with the pressure on the bent elbow, will force your opponent to the ground. How he lands—on his stomach or his back—will determine which lockup to then use.

1: Stepping forward under Kang's arm with his right foot, Master Lee continues to apply pressure to the wrist.

2: He twists his body and kneels on his right knee, throwing Kang.

3: Master Lee maintains his grip on the wrist to allow for a finishing hold.

VARIATION 2: LEG-SCISSOR TAKEDOWN

The leg-scissor take-down becomes an option when the grip on the opponent's hand is compromised or lost. When applying this technique, shoot in deep and attempt to catch his legs between your legs. If you catch only one, do not panic, just continue with the technique. With the proper force and hip positioning, your opponent can be taken down and submitted as long as you have solid control of at least one leg.

1: Maintaining the outside reverse C-lock, Master Lee steps through with his right foot and whips Kang around.

2: Continuing in a circular motion, he drops to the ground and scissors Kang's legs. His right leg is behind Kang's legs, above his knees, and his left leg is in front of Kang's legs, below his knees.

3: Using a clockwise scissor motion with his legs, Master Lee takes Kang to the ground.

STAGE III: GROUND LOCKUP
VARIATION 1: KNEE-ON-NECK SHOULDER QUICK LOCK

This quick lock is used either as a submission or shoulder dislocation. Place your left knee on your opponent's neck and drive your left elbow downward into his shoulder joint while cranking up on his wrist. It is not essential to maintain the C-lock at this point, but it will provide greater

leverage and control. If the C-lock is compromised, you can easily grab his wrist or forearm and still maintain pressure on the shoulder.

1: Master Lee turns Kang's wrist palm-up and reaches underneath his forearm with his left hand.

2: With a twist of the arm, he turns Kang on his side. He places his right hand and left forearm on Kang's elbow, and his shin near Kang's ribs.

3: Master Lee finishes by kneeling across the back of Kang's neck with his left knee, grinding his face into the ground while applying a painful shoulder lock.

VARIATION 2: KNEE COMPRESSION

This knee-separation technique is an excellent follow-up to the leg-scissor takedown. After taking the opponent down, the lower part of your right shin will land in the crook of his knee. Roll toward him and grab his right ankle with your left hand. Continue rolling and reposition his ankle in front of your right hip joint while stepping over his legs with your left foot. This will

allow you to gain control of his upper body by pulling his hair, the lapel of his uniform, or, in a self-defense situation, his neck.

This is a very dangerous technique. In these photos, it is shown as a finishing hold in which the spine is hyperextended and the opponent is set up for a neck-dislocation strike. Or, to submit him, simply acquire a choke and drive your pelvis downward.

1: While turning into Kang, Master Lee grabs Kang's right foot and pushes it up while hooking his right leg behind Kang's knee.

2: Master Lee steps over with his left foot, placing his weight on the back of Kang's knee while locking the ankle in front of his right hip. He sits forward on the leg, compressing the knee.

3: Master Lee finishes by grabbing Kang's hair and pulling his head back, arching the spine and putting pressure on the neck.

OUTSIDE CIRCLE-UNDER
REVERSE C-LOCK   sonmok sangdan hoejon kkokki
손목상단회전격기

EXPLANATION

The outside circle-under reverse C-lock is similar to the inside circle-under C-lock, but it works in the opposite direction. Once again, acquire the two-hand crossed-thumbs grip, but this time spin under the opponent's arm to the outside rather than the inside.

KEY POINTS TO ENHANCE EFFECTIVENESS
STAGE I: ACQUIRING THE GRIP AND ANGLE

Spinning under the arm to the outside will create the proper angle on the opponent's wrist and elbow, and you shouldn't need to use much force. Stepping back with the left foot will cause the elbow to fold and bend farther. Use your thumbs to push on the opponent's wrist while your fingers pull back and downward on his palm. Another option would be to slide your grip down and grab 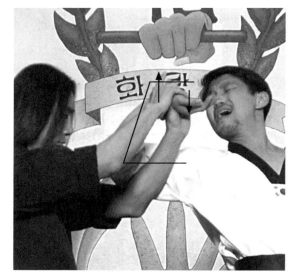 the opponent's fingers to perform a finger crank.

One of the common mistakes with this lock occurs when you try to trap the opponent's elbow in the crook of your arm. This prevents you from applying the sharp angle on the wrist because you are limited by the length of your forearm. By keeping the opponent's elbow outside and free, you have the leverage to direct the wrist all the way to the ground, dropping the opponent.

PUNCH

1: Kang assumes a threatening stance against Master Lee.

2: As Kang throws a right cross, Master Lee steps to the left and deflects the punch with his right forearm.

3: Master Lee quickly grabs the wrist and swings it in a clockwise motion, catching it in his left hand with a top block catch and administering the two-hand thumbs-crossed grip.

LAPEL GRAB

1: Kang grabs Master Lee's lapel with his right hand.

2: Master Lee steps back with his left foot to pull Kang off-balance, and he strikes the pressure point on Kang's wrist to release the grip.

3: Master Lee grabs Kang's wrist, then steps forward and across with his right foot while swinging it downward in a clockwise arc.

WRIST GRAB

1: Kang grabs Master Lee's right wrist with his right hand.

2: Master Lee steps forward with his left foot and brings his right forearm around in a clockwise motion, loosening Kang's grip. He then releases Kang's grip with his left hand.

3: With both hands, Master Lee grabs Kang's hand and swings it down in a clockwise arc.

CHOKE

1: Kang chokes Master Lee with both hands.

2: Master Lee steps back with his right foot to overextend the choke. He grabs Kang's right hand with his left hand and traps it with his right.

3: With a two-hand thumbs-crossed grip, he swings Kang's arm in a clockwise loop.

REAR SHOULDER GRAB

1: Kang grabs Master Lee's right shoulder.

2: Master Lee spins clockwise and grabs Kang's right hand with his left hand and traps it with his right.

3: With a two-hand thumbs-crossed grip, he swings Kang's arm in a clockwise loop.

KNIFE ATTACK

1: Kang threatens Master Lee with an overhead reverse-grip knife attack.

2: As Kang attacks, Master Lee darts outside with his left foot, deflecting Kang's wrist with his right hand.

3: Using the top block catch, Master Lee secures the two-hand thumbs-crossed grip and swings Kang's arm to the outside in a clockwise arc.

115

STAGE II: SETUP AND TAKEDOWN
VARIATION 1: REVERSE C-LOCK TAKEDOWN

The important thing to remember is to place maximum torque on the joints, then drop the opponent's wrist straight down. This is done by stepping back slightly with your left foot and dropping down on the left knee. Sometimes a foot sweep is applied at this stage, but it is unnecessary if the angles on the

wrist are properly applied. This takedown is easy once you understand that it is not a matter of throwing the person, but rather of simply lowering yourself while maintaining the lock on the wrist.

1: Stepping through with his right foot, Master Lee lifts Kang's wrist overhead.

2: He steps around with his left foot, positioning himself behind Kang and securing a painful reverse C-lock.

3: Master Lee steps back and kneels on his left knee, bringing Kang to the ground.

VARIATION 2: WRIST-NECK CONTROL REAR TAKEDOWN

This technique is applied when the opponent counters the takedown by forcing his elbow downward, decreasing the torque on his arm and wrist.

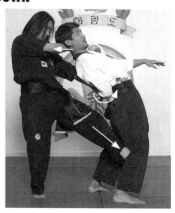

As soon as he attempts to lower his elbow, quickly pull his wrist around his back and grab his left trapezius with your right hand. In doing so, you now control your opponent by forcing him to extend his spine backward. With the addition of a kick to the back of his knee, you further destabilize him and accelerate his fall to the ground.

1. Stepping through with his right foot, Master Lee lifts the wrist overhead.

2. As he spins out, either Kang pulls the arm down or Master Lee forces it downward. Master Lee then places the arm on Kang's back, gaining a shoulder lock with the wrist pinned on Kang's lower back.

3. He then reaches across to Kang's left trapezius with his right hand and pulls him back into a kick behind Kang's right knee.

IMPORTANT THINGS TO REMEMBER

1. Maintain tension on the wrist by pulling it upward along the opponent's spine.

2. Gain control of the neck by pressing on the pressure-point line from the side of the neck down to the area between the trapezius and the collarbone. The best way to acquire this hold is to relax the wrist and let the hand and fingers whip over the shoulder, across the side of the neck. The whipping slap will distract the opponent and cause him to release some of the tension from other muscles, and it will allow you to gain a stronger, deeper hold on the pressure point.

3. To take the opponent down, control his upper body by containing his left shoulder. Kick with your left foot to the back of his right knee while pulling back his wrist with your left hand. This will prevent your opponent from turning as you step back with your left leg and drop to your left knee.

4. As your opponent falls back, you can dislocate his shoulder by pulling his arm straight up.

STAGE III: GROUND LOCKUP
VARIATION 1: UM-YANG REAR POSITION SHOULDER LOCK

This is a shoulder-lock submission. Pin your opponent by sitting on his head while cranking his shoulder. Make sure to go down to one knee and distribute the weight of your body to the left side, where your elbow places pressure on your opponent's shoulder blade. Crank his arm toward your body by curling your left arm and pulling up  with your right. Your right leg is used for balance and leverage.

It is important to sit on his head to maintain control; as long as his head is controlled, you don't have to worry about being rolled over. If he manages to free his head and he rolls into you, however, do not abandon your hold on the arm. You can easily switch your grip to a figure-four hold (see Chapter 8) and obtain a shoulder lock from a different position.

1: While maintaining control of the arm, Master Lee leans forward and drives his left elbow over Kang's elbow, putting his weight on Kang's shoulder.

2: Master Lee scoots his left foot over Kang's head. He then kneels on his left knee and sits on Kang's head, placing his right foot out for support.

3: Grabbing Kang's wrist with both hands, Master Lee places his left forearm on the shoulder while pulling the wrist up, applying a powerful L-lock on the shoulder (see Chapter 7).

VARIATION 2: SHOULDER LOCK FROM REAR MOUNT

In this technique, your opponent's shoulder should have already been hyperextended, if not dislocated, during the takedown. Follow up by using your right arm as a lever to apply greater torque and pressure to his shoulder joint.

For a stronger hold, you can reach with your left hand around his neck to apply a choke. If you clasp your left and right hands together, you'll have a secure lock that creates the double threat of a shoulder dislocation and a choke.

1: Master Lee kneels on his left knee and takes Kang down.

2: Maintaining control of the wrist with his left hand, Master Lee pulls up on the arm as Kang falls, thereby dislocating his shoulder.

3: Master Lee steps over Kang with his right foot and turns him over. He inserts his right forearm into the crook of Kang's elbow and over his shoulder, then torques the shoulder upward.

CHAPTER 7

L-LOCK   mara kkokki   말아꺽기

EXPLANATION

The L-lock is used to dislocate the shoulder. It is a relatively easy technique to administer, but it is not very secure because no grip is involved. The L-lock is applied by intertwining (or "grapevining") your arm around the opponent's, and his bent arm is then used as a lever to create intense torque on the shoulder. To be successful, there must be a very smooth transition between each stage of the technique.

KEY POINTS TO ENHANCE EFFECTIVENESS
STAGE I: ACQUIRING THE GRIP AND ANGLE

To administer the L-lock, shoot your left arm between your opponent's arm and torso, immediately placing your left hand onto the opponent's back. While shooting in with your left arm, shoot your right hand forward to contain the opponent's elbow.

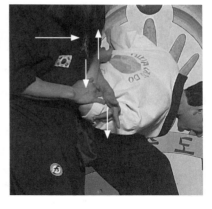

The integrity of the L-lock will be lost if your arm does not remain on the opponent's back, and it is vital that the opponent's hand be immobilized. Once the hold is in place, a common mistake involves placing your hand on the opponent's shoulder and your elbow by the opponent's elbow. This position is easy to counter because the opponent can slip his hand to the front, pull his arm up, and reverse the shoulder lock on you.

Another mistake occurs when you try to force your opponent to bend his elbow with raw muscle power rather than by body positioning. Because you are both standing, the bend of the elbow can be achieved by containing the elbow with the right hand, then sliding your body behind him, carrying his wrist along with you.

Do not try to place the pressure on the shoulder too quickly. The L-angle must be attained before you can effectively apply the shoulder lock, and any premature pressure or tension felt by your opponent means a greater level of resistance from him.

PUNCH

1: Instructor Scott MacKnight (right) threatens Master Lee.

2: As MacKnight punches with a right cross, Master Lee steps to his left and blocks with an inside soft block.

3: Master Lee grabs MacKnight's elbow with his right hand, loops his left forearm around his back, and swings MacKnight forward.

LAPEL GRAB

1: MacKnight grabs Master Lee's lapel and prepares to strike him.

2: Master Lee steps back and pushes diagonally down on MacKnight's hand with his left forearm, loosening the grip.

3: He grabs MacKnight's elbow with his right hand, loops his left forearm around MacKnight's back and swings him forward.

WRIST GRAB

1: MacKnight grabs Master Lee's left wrist with his right hand.

2: Master Lee grabs MacKnight's elbow with his right hand while shooting his left hand toward his back.

3: While controlling the elbow, Master Lee loops his left forearm around MacKnight's back and swings him forward.

CHOKE

1: MacKnight chokes Master Lee from the front.

2: Master Lee lifts his left arm and brings his elbow down on MacKnight's right wrist to break his grip.

3: Continuing with the clockwise motion, he swings his left arm around MacKnight's arm and places it on his lower back while securing the elbow with his right hand.

REAR SHOULDER GRAB

1: MacKnight grabs Master Lee's shoulder from behind.

2: Master Lee spins clockwise on his left foot into MacKnight while striking his hand with his left hand and trapping it with his right arm.

3: Continuing with the clockwise motion, he swings his left arm around MacKnight's arm and places it on his lower back while securing the elbow with his right hand.

KNIFE ATTACK

1: MacKnight threatens Master Lee with a knife.

2: As MacKnight thrusts, Master Lee parries with his left hand with an inside soft block.

3: He snakes his left arm around MacKnight's arm and places it on his lower back while securing the elbow with his right hand.

STAGE II: SETUP AND TAKEDOWN
VARIATION 1: SPINNING OUT

After you've acquired the L-lock, you are ready to take your opponent down. Slide your leg around 180 degrees in a clockwise direction, maintaining the angle with ample torque on the shoulder. Your opponent will be forced to comply with the pain and go down. Drop to your left knee and go to the ground with your opponent, ending up with your left shoulder tightly pressed against his back.

1: Master Lee slides his left arm up and traps MacKnight's wrist in the crook of his elbow.

2: To ensure a tight L-lock, he places his left palm on MacKnight's shoulder while maintaining control of the elbow with his right hand.

3: With a quick 180-degree turn to the right, Master Lee whips MacKnight off his feet and through the air.

VARIATION 2: FLIPPING OVER

This takedown occurs when you apply extreme torque on the shoulder and force your opponent to flip over, or when your opponent tries to roll out of the L-lock. Be sure to maintain the hold on the arm all the way to the ground in order to transition into an effective submission.

1: Master Lee slides his left arm up and traps MacKnight's wrist in the crook of his elbow.

2: Master Lee places his left palm on MacKnight's upper arm, near the elbow.

3: He quickly turns to the right and kneels while dropping his hands and lifting his left elbow, flipping MacKnight.

STAGE III: GROUND LOCKUP
VARIATION 1: REAR MOUNT SHOULDER LOCK

This shoulder lock can be applied as shown or, for a more secure grip, an inside figure-four grip (see Chapter 8) can be used. Push down on the opponent's elbow and raise his wrist up and toward his head. Press your left shoulder down to keep the opponent's hand from escaping the fold of your left arm, and secure his elbow tightly with your right hand.

1: After the takedown, Master Lee maintains the L-lock and presses his body weight on MacKnight.

2: He steps over MacKnight with his right leg.

3: Master Lee pins him on the ground by leaning forward, and he finishes by lifting MacKnight's arm and pulling the shoulder out of joint.

VARIATION 2: GROUND ARMBAR

Your opponent will end up flat on his back, which is ideal for a classic ground armbar. To secure the armbar, remember to maintain control of his arm as he flips though the air.

1: Holding MacKnight's elbow close to his body, Master Lee maintains the OKP.

2: He stands up, steps over MacKnight's head with his left foot, and clamps the arm between his knees.

3: Master Lee falls backward and straightens the arm into a full ground armbar.

CHAPTER 8

FIGURE-FOUR LOCKS   kama kkokki   감아꺾기

OUTSIDE FIGURE-FOUR C-LOCK   sonmok gama kkokki   손목감아꺾기
EXPLANATION

The figure-four lock is one of the most powerful and effective holds. It is versatile and relatively simple to acquire. The goal of all locks is to gain leverage, and the figure-four gives you that ability with ease, because it uses both of your hands against one of your opponent's hands in a grip that works almost like a vice.

With the outside figure-four C-lock, your opponent's hand must be controlled in order to place his wrist at an angle. From this position, the pressure is placed on his wrist and shoulder. This is called the "outside" figure-four in reference to your position in relation to your opponent.

If the grip on his hand is compromised or you initiated the technique by controlling the wrist instead of the hand, the hold would become an outside figure-four L-lock. This is also effective, but it is for dislocating the shoulder and does not apply pressure on the wrist. Using the figure-four L-lock, you can still regain control of the hand, but not from the stand-up position. After the takedown, you can attempt to regain wrist control by acquiring the hand on the ground in Stage III. Furthermore, if your opponent counters by straightening his arm, an armbar can also be applied from the outside figure-four hold.

KEY POINTS TO ENHANCE EFFECTIVENESS
STAGE I: ACQUIRING THE GRIP AND ANGLE

This hold can be easily obtained with an outside/inside catch. The entry into the technique is the same as the two-hand outside C-lock.

The important concept to remember is that you must grip your own wrist near your hand and not farther up the forearm. The goal is to gain greater leverage on the opponent's arm for maximum control, and the opponent's elbow is contained and controlled by your forearm.

PUNCH

1: Kang prepares to strike Master Lee.

2: As Kang fires a right cross, Master Lee sidesteps to the left and performs an outside/inside catch.

3: Master Lee grabs Kang's hand with his right hand, then loops his left arm over his elbow, bending it back. He bends Kang's wrist and grabs his own forearm with his left hand, creating a figure-four C-lock.

LAPEL GRAB

1: Kang grabs Master Lee's lapel with his right hand.

2: Master Lee steps to the right and performs an outside/inside catch, loosening Kang's grip.

3: Master Lee grabs Kang's hand with his right hand, then loops his left arm over his elbow, bending it back. He bends Kang's wrist and grabs his own forearm with his left hand, creating a figure-four C-lock.

WRIST GRAB

1: Kang grabs Master Lee's right wrist with his right hand.

2: Bringing both his hands around Kang's arm in a clockwise loop, Master Lee secures Kang's wrist and elbow.

3: Master Lee grabs Kang's hand with his right hand, then loops his left arm over his elbow, bending it back. He bends Kang's wrist and grabs his own forearm with his left hand, creating a figure-four C-lock.

CHOKE

1: Kang chokes Master Lee with both hands.

2: Master Lee steps back with his right foot while bringing his left elbow over Kang's right arm. He simultaneously grabs Kang's right hand using the outside/inside catch.

3: As Kang's arm recoils, Master Lee bends Kang's wrist and arm and grabs his right forearm, securing the figure-four C-lock.

131

REAR SHOULDER GRAB

1: Kang grabs Master Lee's shoulder from behind.

2: Master Lee spins on his right foot and dislodges Kang's grip.

3: Master Lee grabs Kang's hand with his right hand, then loops his left arm over his elbow, bending it back. He bends Kang's wrist and grabs his own forearm with his left hand, creating a figure-four C-lock.

KNIFE ATTACK

1: Kang menaces Master Lee with a knife, held in a reverse grip.

2: As Kang slashes down at his face, Master Lee sidesteps and deflects the forearm with both hands, using an outside/inside catch.

3: Master Lee grabs Kang's right wrist, controlling the weapon. He then loops his left arm over Kang's elbow and bends it back. He bends Kang's wrist and grabs his own forearm with his left hand, creating a figure-four C-lock. This puts the blade dangerously close to Kang's neck and face, and Master Lee can cut him if necessary.

STAGE II: SETUP AND TAKEDOWN
VARIATION 1: TAKEDOWN WITH A STEP THROUGH

This is a more aggressive attack in which you step through and throw your opponent's upper body off-balance. The takedown is applied by applying downward pressure to his arm and dropping to the OKP. Remember to maintain the figure-four at all times.

1: Master Lee steps through with his right foot, putting more pressure on the wrist and shoulder.

2: He kneels on his left knee and throws Kang.

3: Master Lee maintains the figure-four lock.

VARIATION 2: TAKEDOWN WITH A STEP BACK

The stepping-back takedown can be applied when your opponent pulls his arms in and resists your outside push. Follow his momentum by stepping forward with your right leg, and redirect his force by crossing over with your left foot into a back step and dropping to the knee. This is a pulling takedown, whereas the previous technique was a pushing takedown. It is important in both techniques to maintain a firm grip at all times.

1: Kang resists and pulls his arm inward. Master Lee steps forward with his right leg, then back with his left leg.

2: Master Lee twists and kneels.

3: Kang is thrown by the tremendous leverage created by the proper footwork and positioning.

STAGE III: GROUND LOCKUP
VARIATION 1: KNEE-ON-NECK WRIST QUICK LOCK

This is another wrist quick lock. With a figure-four hold, however, it becomes much more secure and gives you greater leverage. Note that both of your hands should pull in with no space anywhere for your opponent to wriggle or maneuver his arm for a potential escape. Everything is very compact and held close to the body. Be sure to place constant pressure on the neck and sit up, pushing your hip and chest forward, placing additional painful pressure on the wrist. Additionally,

make sure the right hand is focused on the opponent's hand rather than the wrist.

1: Master Lee maintains the figure-four lock and scoots forward.

2: He drops his shin across Kang's face and cranks back the wrist. Note that Kang's elbow is pinned against Master Lee's biceps and trapped in the fold of his arm.

VARIATION 2: GROUND ARMBAR

If the hand slips out and the wrist lock is compromised, you are set up perfectly to finish with a ground armbar.

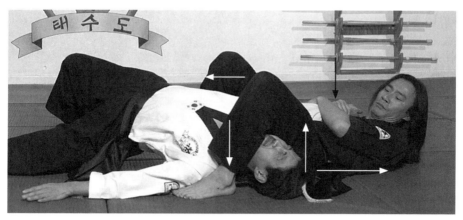

1: Master Lee slides his right leg next to Kang's ribs.

2: He steps over Kang's face with his left foot.

3: Master Lee sits back and secures the armbar. By holding the arm securely to his chest and arching his back, Master Lee will hyperextend the elbow.

INSIDE FIGURE-FOUR L-LOCK kumch'i gama kkokki
굼치감아꺽기

EXPLANATION

This technique works similarly to the outside figure-four, but it is applied from the inside of the opponent. It is especially applicable when your opponent grabs around your waist from the rear in either a standing position or on the ground. This lock focuses on the elbow and/or shoulder, and acquiring the hand to control the wrist is not necessary. If your opponent straightens his arm, apply an armbar from the figure-four grip. If his arm is bent, apply the shoulder lock.

KEY POINTS TO ENHANCE EFFECTIVENESS
STAGE I: ACQUIRING THE GRIP AND ANGLE

The figure-four can be acquired with a top block catch or in any situation in which the wrist is available for you to acquire a grip. Immediately wrap your other arm over and under your opponent's arm and acquire a grip on your own wrist in a figure-four fashion. This is necessary in order to gain the "two hands versus one" leverage.

Squeezing the opponent's wrist places additional pressure against the bone and nerves. This is done by pushing your right wrist and forearm outward while pulling your opponent's hand inward with your left hand. This adds more pain to the wrist and gives you tighter control of the opponent's arm.

PUNCH

1: Kang prepares to strike Master Lee.

2: The block is deflected by a left outward knifehand (or outside soft block) as Master Lee moves in with his right foot.

3: Master Lee grabs the wrist with his left hand, wraps his right arm over Kang's and grabs his own wrist, securing the figure-four grip.

LAPEL GRAB

1: Kang grabs Master Lee's lapel with his right hand.

2: Master Lee spins counterclockwise into Kang, bringing his right arm over Kang's and trapping it. He then peels Kang's hand off his lapel and administers the figure-four grip.

3: Master Lee turns clockwise, administering pressure to the shoulder.

WRIST GRAB

1: Kang grabs Master Lee's left wrist with his right hand.

2: Master Lee steps in with his right foot and, making a small counterclockwise circle with his left hand, grabs Kang's wrist.

3: He arcs his right arm over Kang's and secures the figure-four grip.

CHOKE

1: Kang chokes Master Lee with both hands.

2: Master Lee steps back with his left foot, pulling Kang's wrist with his left hand while shooting his right arm up.

3: He smashes his elbow down on Kang's arms while pivoting, swinging his right arm over and around Kang's arms. He then administers the figure-four grip.

REAR SHOULDER GRAB

1: Kang grabs Master Lee's shoulder from behind.

2: Master Lee pivots on his right foot to face Kang. He grabs his wrist with his left hand while shooting his right hand into the air, preparing to slam downward to release the grip.

3: He steps forward with his right foot, loops his arm over and around Kang's and applies the figure-four grip.

KNIFE ATTACK

1: Kang threatens Master Lee with a knife.

2: As Kang steps in and swings the blade toward Master Lee's head, he sidesteps and blocks with his left hand.

3: Master Lee grabs Kang's hand, loops his arm over and around Kang's and applies the figure-four grip, keeping the knife in a safe position.

STAGE II: SETUP AND TAKEDOWN
VARIATION 1: STEPPING OUT

Once you've secured the figure-four hold, the takedown is easy to apply. Simply step out on the same side with which you are placing pressure downward with the shoulder (in this case, with the right leg). Make sure to bridge your hip up and keep all your weight on the right side of your body.

The effectiveness of the takedown will be determined by how deeply you step out with your right leg and how much downward pressure you apply with your upper body. The pressure will either be on your opponent's elbow (if his arm is straight) or on his shoulder (if his arm is bent).

These concepts require some basic knowledge of groundwork, but for now just remember that your mobility is limited when you place your hips flat on the ground. Be sure to land on the ground on your right side and not flat on your back. Being on one hip allows greater mobility to turn and take your opponent's back.

1: Master Lee positions Kang's arm in an elbow-up position and kicks his right leg forward, dropping his weight on Kang's shoulder and arm.

2: Kang drops to the floor with the grip firmly in place. To apply the submission, Master Lee uses his armpit to apply pressure on Kang's upper arm while lifting up on his wrist.

141

VARIATION 2: WITH INSIDE SWEEP

The sweep can be applied when stepping out is not enough to take your opponent down. If it degrades into a struggle and you need to offset your opponent's balance, a simple inside sweep with your right foot to his shin just above the ankle will do the trick, and he will be unable to counter your takedown.

The important thing to remember is to maintain constant pressure on your opponent's shoulder by driving your weight and right elbow into his shoulder and lifting your arms up. The takedown trajectory is similar to a side fall. The right leg kicks up the opponent's leg, as if you were breakfalling by slapping down on your opponent's back. If he turns toward you and lands on his back, do not panic. As long as you have maintained the figure-four hold on the arm, you can acquire the shoulder lock from any position on the ground with a little knowledge of groundwork.

1: Master Lee lifts Kang's wrist, forcing him to lean forward.

2: Master Lee continues forcing Kang down and positions his right foot next to Kang's.

3: He takes Kang down by sweeping in the opposite direction.

STAGE III: GROUND LOCKUP
VARIATION 1: SHOULDER LOCK FROM REAR MOUNT

While taking your opponent down, place constant downward pressure and torque on his shoulder. Remember to land on your right side and be prepared to take your opponent's back. To take his back, you must prevent your opponent from lifting his shoulder off the ground. It must be pinned so you can use it as a

pivot point when you push off with your left leg and mount the back.

After you have successfully mounted, it is easy to submit him with a shoulder lock. Just curl your left biceps and lift the opponent's hand as you dig your elbow into the inside of his biceps. Then drive everything toward the opponent's head by pushing up with your left arm and hip. Also, the left leg can be used to push off to help raise the opponent's hand for a more extreme angle on the shoulder.

It is important to keep your opponent from squirming around. This is accomplished by applying the proper force downward on his arm with your elbow and biceps curl. You can further ensure stabilization by dropping down to both knees and sitting on him with all your weight. Then, by

1: Master Lee follows his twisting momentum and leans over Kang's locked arm.

2: He slides up and steps over Kang with his left leg for additional leverage.

3: Master Lee leans forward and applies the painful shoulder submission.

squeezing your legs, you pin your opponent's hip in place and push yourself upward toward his head.

If your opponent tries to push off with his free hand, simply snatch it up and bring it to the rear, acquiring a double-rear shoulder lock. For complete immobilization, you can pull the hair back and acquire a choke or head control.

VARIATION 2: SHOULDER LOCK FROM SIDE MOUNT

Often, your opponent will try to turn to face you. If this happens, do not panic. You can acquire the shoulder lock from the side-mount position. Make sure to maintain the figure-four grip, and shift your hip up toward your opponent's head. This will  increase the pressure on his shoulder and raise his upper body. This alone might be enough for a submission, but for greater control and stabilization, it is best to wrap your right leg over and around the opponent's head to lock him in position.

1: Kang turns, and Master Lee maintains his hold and secures a side-mount position.

2: He slides his left hip up toward Kang's head, which forces Kang's arm back and raises his back off the ground.

3: To make the hold more secure, Master Lee wraps his right leg over Kang's head while twisting his arm back and up.

CHAPTER 9

WRIST-ELBOW-SHOULDER (WES) LOCK samdam kkokki 삼단꺾기

EXPLANATION

The wrist-elbow-shoulder (WES) lock is essentially a C-lock with L-lock components. It has great leverage and places extreme pressure and angles on the wrist, shoulder and, to a lesser extent, the elbow. In this hold, the weakest joint will dislocate first. Slight variations in angles and manipulation will shift the maximum pressure from one joint to another. If you lose your grip on your opponent's hand, you still have an L-lock that can be used to dislocate the shoulder as long as you have control of the wrist.

KEY POINTS TO ENHANCE EFFECTIVENESS
STAGE I: ACQUIRING THE GRIP AND ANGLE

To apply the WES lock, you must first obtain the traditional C-lock. The added use of your right forearm to strike inward at the opponent's elbow while pushing with your left makes it a very aggressive approach. As soon as you strike his midarm with your right arm, you must redirect your right hand and pull down on his hand while lifting up your forearm to raise the opponent's elbow. This creates an extreme angle on the shoulder.

Be sure to maintain the 90-degree angle on the elbow. However, if your opponent compromises the angle of his elbow by forcing his arm straighter, an armbar can be applied by pulling and extending his arm and then striking his extended elbow with your shoulder. This is a viable alternative as long as you have maintained control over his hand to keep the elbow pointed inward with a C-lock. If you lose your grip with your left hand, you must either abandon and escape or move into a clinch.

145

PUNCH

1: Kang prepares to strike Master Lee.

2: Master Lee steps back with his right foot and secures Kang's hand with an overhand grab.

3: Master Lee steps through with his right foot, twisting Kang's arm outward while inserting his forearm in the crook of Kang's elbow. Lifting the arm while twisting down on the wrist creates immense pressure on the wrist, elbow and shoulder.

LAPEL GRAB

1: Kang grabs Master Lee's lapel with his right hand.

2: Stepping back with his right foot, Master Lee grabs Kang's hand with his left hand and brings his other hand around to the outside of the grip.

3: Master Lee steps through with his right foot, twisting Kang's arm outward while inserting his forearm in the crook of Kang's elbow. Lifting the arm while twisting down on the wrist creates immense pressure on the wrist, elbow and shoulder.

WRIST GRAB

1: Kang grabs Master Lee's right wrist with his right hand.

2: Master Lee turns his right hand in a counterclockwise arc, weakening Kang's grip, and grabs Kang's hand with his left hand.

3: Master Lee steps through with his right foot, twisting Kang's arm outward while inserting his forearm in the crook of Kang's elbow. Lifting the arm while twisting down on the wrist creates immense pressure on the wrist, elbow and shoulder.

CHOKE

1: Kang chokes Master Lee with both hands.

2: Stepping back with his right foot, Master Lee grabs Kang's hand with his left hand and brings his other hand around to the outside of the grip, preparing for the WES lock.

3: Master Lee steps through with his right foot, twisting Kang's arm outward while inserting his forearm in the crook of Kang's elbow. Lifting the arm while twisting down on the wrist creates immense pressure on the wrist, elbow and shoulder.

REAR SHOULDER GRAB

1: Kang grabs Master Lee's shoulder from behind.

2: Master Lee spins on his right foot, weakening Kang's grip, and grabs his hand with his left hand while positioning his right hand for the WES lock.

3: Master Lee steps through with his right foot, twisting Kang's arm outward while inserting his forearm in the crook of Kang's elbow. Lifting the arm while twisting down on the wrist creates immense pressure on the wrist, elbow and shoulder.

KNIFE ATTACK

1: Kang threatens Master Lee with a knife.

2: As Kang lunges forward, Master Lee sidesteps to the right and secures the hand with a left overhand grab.

3: Master Lee steps through with his right foot, twisting Kang's arm outward while inserting his forearm in the crook of Kang's elbow. Lifting the arm while twisting down on the wrist creates immense pressure on the wrist, elbow and shoulder.

STAGE II: SETUP AND TAKEDOWN

As you swing your right hand down onto your opponent's twisted wrist, you must drop down into the OKP, maintaining the lift on his elbow by lifting up your right elbow. Make sure your opponent's hand is twisted inward, weakening the elbow further and preventing him from straightening his arm. The takedown will be lost if the angle at the elbow is lost. This is why you should not drag the arm away from him horizontally; instead, drop it straight down to the ground as the arrow indicates.

1: By kneeling and pulling down on the wrist with both hands while pushing up on the elbow with his forearm, Master Lee creates even more pressure on all three joints.

2: Kang has no choice but to vault over.

3: Master Lee maintains his grip after Kang falls.

STAGE III: GROUND LOCKUP
VARIATION 1: INSIDE KNEE-ON-NECK SHOULDER QUICK LOCK

This works the same way as the inside knee-on-neck wrist lock, except now you are cranking the arm outside to your left to dislocate the elbow and/or shoulder. Stomp on his face, then enter into the inside knee-on-neck lock.

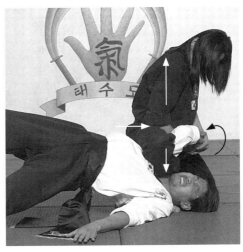

1: Master Lee steps over with his right foot and stomps on Kang's face while maintaining the WES lock.

2: He slides his foot beneath Kang's neck and braces Kang's elbow against his inner thigh.

3: Master Lee torques Kang's wrist outward with both hands, dislocating the shoulder.

VARIATION 2: OUTSIDE KNEE-ON-NECK SHOULDER QUICK LOCK

Essentially, this works the same as the previously mentioned technique, except you place the left knee on the opponent's neck without stepping over. This is less stable than the inside knee-on-neck shoulder lock, but easier and faster to acquire. In both instances, the effectiveness of the technique comes from maintaining the WES grip.

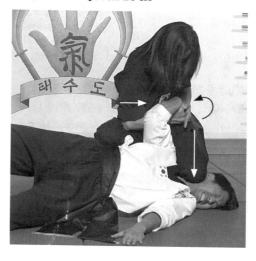

The dislocation of the elbow occurs when you turn your entire torso and hip to the outside (or counterclockwise, in this case). Also, pushing forward with your right hip will add greatly to the tension on the shoulder. If his head slips out, you can simply transition by placing your right knee on the right side of his chest, pinning his shoulder to the ground.

1: While maintaining the WES lock, Master Lee digs his thumb into the pressure point beneath Kang's jaw line, thereby forcing his head down and exposing his neck.

2: Master Lee slides his left shin forward and kneels onto the base of Kang's skull.

3: While keeping Kang's head pinned, Master Lee torques his wrist outward with both hands, tearing the neck and shoulder muscles.

CIRCLE-UNDER WES   samdan hoejon kkokki   삼단회전꺾기

EXPLANATION

This is the same as the standard WES, but with a circle-under entry. The WES angle is achieved during the rotation under the opponent's arm

KEY POINTS TO ENHANCE EFFECTIVENESS
STAGE I: ACQUIRING THE GRIP AND ANGLE

It is important to remember to bend the wrist by moving your whole body, not by using only the strength of your hand. Take control of his elbow, push it away from you, and step in to acquire the 90-degree angle on the wrist. Bending the opponent's wrist at the outset of the technique is very important. From this point, step through toward your opponent's left side and spin to your right to apply the lock.

After you have spun under his arm, you should have the WES lock, with right angles on the wrist and on the elbow. Be sure to maintain contact and upward pressure with your forearm on the opponent's elbow at all times.

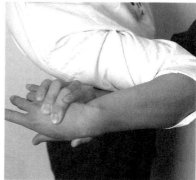

PUNCH

1: Kang prepares to strike Master Lee.

2: Master Lee sidesteps to the right and executes a left knifehand block.

3: He steps back with his left foot, swings the punch counterclockwise, and catches Kang's wrist in his right hand with a top block catch.

LAPEL GRAB

1: Kang grabs Master Lee's lapel with his right hand.

2: Master Lee twists his body and grabs Kang's wrist from underneath with his right hand.

3: He quickly steps back with his left foot, pulling Kang off-balance, and brings his left hand over Kang's hand, peeling it loose.

WRIST GRAB

1: Kang grabs Master Lee's wrist with his right hand.

2: With his left hand, Master Lee grabs the pressure point in the crease of Kang's elbow, causing him to loosen his grip.

3: Still applying pressure, Master Lee moves to his right and bends Kang's arm and wrist inward, securing his wrist with his right hand.

CHOKE

1: Kang chokes Master Lee with both hands.

2: Master Lee slams his forearm down on Kang's left elbow, breaking the grip.

3: Master Lee steps back with his left foot and grabs Kang's right wrist with his right hand.

REAR SHOULDER GRAB

1: Kang grabs Master Lee's shoulder from behind.

2: Master Lee spins clockwise. He slaps Kang's hand away with his left hand and prepares to catch it in his right.

3: As he catches Kang's hand, Master Lee whips Kang's arm around in a counterclockwise arc.

KNIFE ATTACK

1: Kang threatens Master Lee with an overhead knife attack.

2: As Kang stabs downward, Master Lee sidesteps to the right and deflects the attack with his left forearm.

3: He swings Kang's hand down into a two-hand thumbs-crossed grip using the top block catch.

STAGE II: SETUP AND TAKEDOWN
VARIATION 1: WES TAKEDOWN

Once the proper grip and angles are acquired, you are ready for the takedown. Do not raise the opponent's arm too high; instead, create just enough space to shoot under. Take care to prevent your spine from arching backward, and do not lift your hands too high or too far back behind your head. Once you have stepped through, quickly turn and drop to the OKP on the left knee.

A common mistake with this technique is to use it as a shoulder crank by pulling down on the opponent's hand with both of your hands. However, that is a separate technique which is applied without torquing the angle of the wrist. In the WES takedown, you must bridge your opponent's elbow on your forearm and use your left hand not to pull down on his arm but to keep his elbow in place.

1: Master Lee steps out slightly with his right foot to create space while maintaining control of the wrist and elbow.

2: He steps under Kang's arm with his left foot.

3: Master Lee kneels on his left knee while holding the arm securely in the WES lock, and Kang is thrown.

156

VARIATION 2: ARMBAR-DRAG FORWARD SWEEP

If you have a firm hold on the hand and maintain the angle on the wrist, it is very difficult for your opponent to counter by straightening his arm. However, if he is strong enough to outmuscle you and is able to straighten the arm, don't worry. You will be in perfect position to execute an armbar with your shoulder while sweeping out the rear leg with an outside sweep.

To execute the armbar-drag forward sweep, simply drag his arm across your body and drive your right shoulder all the way to the ground in order to take him down. You must make sure to keep your head down, your body bent forward, and your hips pushed back in order to keep from falling backward as you apply the sweep. Always balance on the balls of your feet, especially in this situation, because it is easy to lose your balance.

Another point to remember is to sweep higher on his leg, by his knee, when applying a forward sweep. If the sweep is below the knee, your opponent will easily avoid it by lifting his foot and bending his leg.

1: Master Lee steps out slightly with his right foot to create space while maintaining control of the wrist and elbow.

2: Kang counters by straightening his arm, and Master Lee steps all the way around with his left leg and places his right shoulder firmly against Kang's elbow.

3: Master Lee performs an outside sweep to the inside of Kang's rear leg while dropping his weight and maintaining pressure on the elbow, thereby throwing Kang.

157

STAGE III: GROUND LOCKUP
VARIATION 1: SHOULDER QUICK LOCK WITH A WES GRIP

This is very easy to apply. Simply press down on your opponent's elbow, forcing it against his temple. To finish the submission, lift his hand while maintaining the angle on his wrist. Owing to the nature of the WES grip, it is possible to dislocate the shoulder, the elbow and/or the wrist at the same time.

1: After the takedown, Master Lee maintains control of the elbow and wrist.

2: He pushes Kang's elbow down toward his face.

3: Master Lee applies the submission by lifting Kang's wrist while holding the elbow down, severely damaging the shoulder.

VARIATION 2: ELBOW QUICK LOCK WITH A WES GRIP

This lock is applied when your opponent rolls onto his stomach. Maintaining the WES grip, secure his elbow with your left hand and press it firmly to the ground. Quickly replace your left hand with your left knee and assist your right-hand grip on the opponent's hand with your left hand. Drop all your body weight onto his biceps and lift the hand. You must

keep the elbow stationary with your knee in order to dislocate the elbow. Because the shoulder is pinned down, this submission will not dislocate the shoulder.

1: As Kang hits the floor, Master Lee maintains control of his wrist.

2: He follows Kang's momentum and pins his elbow to the floor with his left hand.

3: Master Lee places his left shin in the crook of Kang's elbow and pulls up on his wrist, dislocating the wrist and/or elbow.

CHAPTER 10

OUTSIDE WRIST TWIST   oe sonmok doryu kkokki
외손목돌려꺾기

EXPLANATION

This outside wrist twist is a transitional technique that can be used to set up many different locks using the hand and wrist grip.

KEY POINTS TO ENHANCE EFFECTIVENESS
STAGE I: ACQUIRING THE GRIP AND THE ANGLE

This is a leveraged-angle attack. Your right hand secures the opponent's hand and rotates it away from you in a clockwise direction, placing pressure on his wrist. Your left hand keeps his arm stable and assists in the direction you wish to move the opponent. This lock itself is not enough to secure a takedown, and it must be used in conjunction with additional techniques to take your opponent down and submit him.

PUNCH

1: Kang prepares to strike Master Lee.

2: Master Lee sidesteps and parries the punch with his left hand.

3: He follows the momentum of the parry and carries the punch around in a clockwise loop. Using the cross-down block catch, he traps the hand.

LAPEL GRAB

1: Kang grabs Master Lee's lapel with his right hand.

2: Master Lee covers Kang's hand with his right palm and steps back with his left foot, pulling Kang off-balance and loosening his grip.

3: Maintaining control of the hand, Master Lee grabs Kang's wrist with his left hand and twists both clockwise.

WRIST GRAB

1: Kang grabs Master Lee's wrist.

2: Master Lee loops his hand clockwise, hooking Kang's wrist between his thumb and index finger.

3: Continuing the loop, Master Lee traps Kang's hand with his right hand.

CHOKE

1: Kang chokes Master Lee.

2: Master Lee steps back with his left foot while grabbing Kang's right wrist from below with his left hand. He simultaneously grabs Kang's right hand from above with his right hand.

3: He steps out with his right foot, twisting Kang's arm clockwise.

REAR SHOULDER GRAB

1: Kang grabs Master Lee's shoulder from behind.

2: Master Lee spins counterclockwise and strikes Kang's thumb with his right hand, knocking his hand away. He grabs Kang's wrist with his left hand.

3: Grabbing Kang's hand with his right hand and maintaining control of the wrist, Master Lee steps out with his right foot and twists the arm clockwise.

KNIFE ATTACK

1: Kang, holding the knife in a forward grip, prepares to attack Master Lee.

2: As Kang thrusts, Master Lee slides back with his right foot and blocks with a cross-down block catch, grabbing Kang's hand with his right hand.

3: Master Lee grabs Kang's wrist with his left hand and prepares to twist the arm clockwise.

STAGE II: SETUP AND TAKEDOWN
VARIATION 1: FRONT-KICK STRAIGHT-ARM WRIST PULL DOWN

With the opponent's body bent at the waist, you are in perfect position to deliver a kick. You can kick with either leg, but it is better to use your outside leg. If you use your inside leg, your opponent's leg might get in the way and, at best, you might kick his ribs or midsection. Kicks with the outside leg, however, are unobstructed, and the face (a more lethal target)  becomes vulnerable. After the kick, which should loosen any tension, step back and drag your opponent to the ground by the wrist.

1: Master Lee continues the clockwise arc, forcing Kang to bend down.

2: He delivers a right kick to Kang's face, stunning him.

3: Master Lee immediately steps back with his right foot while pulling the arm back and pushing down on the wrist, bending it painfully backward.

VARIATION 2: KNEE-ON-ARM TAKEDOWN

This takedown is executed by placing your shin over the back of the opponent's upper arm and driving your knee and shin toward the ground while lifting up on his hand. Remember that you must place your shin more on his arm than on his shoulder, and keep his elbow from bending backward by rotating his hand clockwise with his fingers pointing upward. This ensures that his elbow is also pointing up, preventing him from bending the arm to counter the pressure on his elbow.

If his elbow bends somehow, you can transition to a shoulder lock. Continue to drive downward, but put pressure on his shoulder rather than his elbow. This is more likely to cause your opponent to try to roll out, in which case other ground locks are available.

1: Master Lee continues the clockwise arc, forcing Kang to bend down.

2: He lifts his left knee, preparing to drop it on Kang's shoulder. (Avoid raising the knee too high and losing your balance.)

3: Master Lee bring his knee and shin down on Kang's shoulder and triceps, forcing him to the ground.

165

STAGE III: GROUND LOCKUP
VARIATION 1: KNEE-ON-SHOULDER-BLADE QUICK LOCK

This is a relatively simple lock. After your opponent is taken to the ground, quickly place your left knee on his shoulder blade while maintaining full control of his arm. Prevent it from bending by securing his wrist and forearm between your legs. To dislocate and increase the tension on his shoulder, drive your hip forward over his head. Be sure to bring your right leg up by his head  and squeeze your legs inward to secure his arm.

1: After Kang goes to the ground, Master Lee maintains his grip on the hand and pins the shoulder by pushing down and bending the wrist.

2: Master Lee slides his left knee around and onto Kang's shoulder blade, pinning Kang's entire upper body to the ground.

3: He slides his right foot toward Kang's head and brings his knee inward to secure Kang's arm. He then drives his hip forward to dislocate the shoulder.

VARIATION 2: KNEE-ON-TRICEPS ELBOW QUICK LOCK

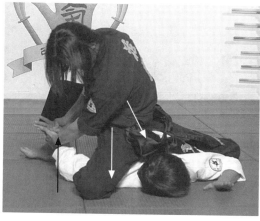

Though securing an armbar from this position is possible, it is not the best option with this particular grip. However, by sitting on your opponent's back and pressing down on his triceps with your left shin, you can pin his shoulder and elbow on the mat and inflict excruciating pain to his upper arm. The elbow and shoulder can be dislocated simply by bending his arm at the elbow and raising his hand up and forward.

1: Master Lee sits on Kang's upper back, pinning him on the ground, while leaning on his upper arm with his shin and maintaining control of the wrist.

2: By bending the arm at a right angle and lifting up, Master Lee can easily tear the tendons in Kang's shoulder and elbow.

CHAPTER 11

S-LOCK   kakto kkokki   각도꺾기

EXPLANATION

The S-lock is basically a wrist twist with a bent elbow. The entry into the S-lock is the same as the wrist twist, and they both work in conjunction with each other, both using the hand and wrist grip.

KEY POINTS TO ENHANCE EFFECTIVENESS
STAGE I: ACQUIRING THE GRIP AND ANGLE

You can either respond with the S-lock if your opponent counters the wrist twist or use the wrist twist to obtain the S-lock. For now, we will address how to obtain the S-lock proactively.

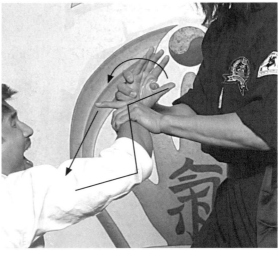

What defines the S-lock is the 90-degree angle of the opponent's elbow, which can be attained simply by twisting his hand inward and stepping toward him. The wrist twist will loosen the elbow and allow you to acquire the angle. Continue to drive his hand and wrist down and inward toward his stomach. This should bring your opponent to his knees and set him up for the takedown.

PUNCH

1: Kang prepares to strike Master Lee.

2: Master Lee steps back with his right foot and parries with an inside soft block.

3: He shoots his right forearm below Kang's wrist and forearm, using the inside/outside catch.

LAPEL GRAB

1: Kang grabs Master Lee's lapel with his right hand.

2: Master Lee steps back with his left foot and covers Kang's hand with his right palm.

3: He grabs Kang's wrist with his left hand and uses the combined pressure from both hands to bend the wrist and release the grip.

WRIST GRAB

1: Kang grabs Master Lee's right wrist with his right hand.

2: Master Lee swings his wrist around Kang's in a clockwise loop.

3: As Master Lee's right hand comes over Kang's wrist at the apex of the loop, Master Lee pins Kang's fingers with his left hand, preventing escape.

CHOKE

1: Kang chokes Master Lee with both hands.

2: Master Lee steps back with his left foot while reaching across and grabbing Kang's right hand with his right hand. He simultaneously grabs Kang's right wrist from underneath with his left hand.

3: By rotating Kang's hand and wrist down and clockwise, Master Lee drops Kang to his knee.

REAR SHOULDER GRAB

1: Kang grabs Master Lee's shoulder from behind.

2: Master Lee quickly spins clockwise and grabs Kang's wrist with his left hand. He inserts his right thumb in the webbing between Kang's thumb and index finger and wraps his fingers around the hand, establishing a tight grip.

3: By rotating Kang's hand and wrist down and clockwise, Master Lee drops Kang to his knee.

KNIFE ATTACK

1: Kang threatens Master Lee with a knife.

2: As Kang thrusts the knife, Master Lee sidesteps and deflects the blow with the cross-down block catch.

3: By placing opposing pressure on Kang's wrist, he applies an S-lock and weakens Kang's grip on the knife.

STAGE II: SETUP AND TAKEDOWN
VARIATION 1: KNEE-TO-FACE TAKEDOWN

After your opponent has gone down to one knee, simply step back with your right foot, pulling him forward and off-balance, and then deliver your right knee to his face. Make sure to maintain your grip and the angles on his wrist and elbow. (In this photo, the hand position is slightly different because this S-lock was acquired from a defense against a wrist grab.)

1: Master Lee applies the S-lock by snaking his right hand over Kang's wrist, driving it inward and down, while holding the fingers in place with his left hand to prevent escape.

2: He steps back with his right foot while maintaining the S-lock.

3: Master Lee shoots his right knee into Kang's face.

VARIATION 2: SITTING ARMBAR TAKEDOWN

This technique is applied when your opponent counters by stepping back and straightening the arm. Bring your left leg over his arm and sit on his upper arm, above the elbow, while lifting his wrist with both hands. Arch your body backward to place additional stress on his elbow. Be sure to maintain constant contact with your buttocks on the opponent's arm. If any pressure is lost, your opponent can counter by simply bending his arm. If this happens, transition to a shoulder lock.

1: Master Lee steps back with his right foot and pulls the arm straight.

2: He swings his left leg over the arm and sits slightly above the elbow.

3: By dropping into a kneeling position, Master Lee slams Kang to the floor.

STAGE III: GROUND LOCKUP
VARIATION 1: KNEE-ON-NECK QUICK S-LOCK

When you knee your opponent's face, your right foot will end up on his left side. Simply kneel down across his neck with your right shin as if it were a guillotine, firmly planting your knee above his right shoulder.

Maintaining the S-lock grip, drive his hand forward as you sit back, and press downward on his wrist. For better control, hold his biceps tightly against your right inner thigh to keep it from moving around.

1: After kneeing Kang, Master Lee's shin is poised above his throat while he maintains the S-lock.

2: He drops his shin and pins Kang to the ground while bending his arm over his leg.

3: Master Lee finishes by amplifying the torque of the S-lock and driving his body weight down and forward.

VARIATION 2: SITTING ARMBAR

After you've stepped over the arm, the lock is as simple as sitting in a chair. The important thing to keep in mind is that you must keep your weight back at the opponent's shoulder joint rather than at his upper arm. This provides better stability and added pressure. If your opponent manages to roll back into you and you fall to your back, you are in a good position to administer a ground armbar.

1: To finish Kang off, Master Lee bends his left leg, trapping Kang's arm at the shoulder, while sitting on his upper back.

2: He lifts the arm straight up, breaking it at the elbow.

REVERSE S-LOCK   yokkakto kkokki   역각도꺽기

EXPLANATION

The reverse S-lock is a compression technique, since the wrist will only bend back to a certain angle before the joint starts to separate. We are not using the reverse S-lock as a wrist crank (as is commonly seen) but rather as a setup for a shoulder dislocation.

KEY POINTS TO ENHANCE EFFECTIVENESS
STAGE I: ACQUIRING THE GRIP AND ANGLE

The grip and setup are similar to the standard wrist crank. Gain control of your opponent's left hand on the palm side with your right hand, and bend his elbow with your left hand. By spinning counterclockwise on your right foot and bringing the opponent's arm over your shoulder, you end up in the reverse S-lock position. Push his elbow away with your left hand and pull inward and downward with your right hand. This will dislocate the shoulder and put you in position for a wrist crank.

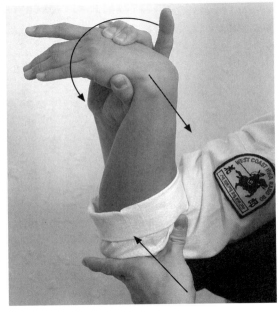

PUNCH

1: Kang prepares to strike Master Lee.

2: As Kang punches, Master Lee sidesteps to the right and blocks with a left outward knifehand or outside soft block.

3: He grabs Kang's wrist with his left hand and, with a top block catch, swings it downward and counterclockwise. Master Lee catches it with his right hand in an inverted handshake, covering Kang's thumb with his fingers.

LAPEL GRAB

1: Kang grabs Master Lee's lapel with his left hand.

2: Master Lee steps back with his left foot, pulling Kang off-balance, while grabbing the underside of Kang's hand with his left hand. He strikes Kang's thumb with his right hand to release the grip.

3: Holding Kang's left wrist with his right hand, Master Lee swings it downward and counterclockwise. He catches it with his right hand in an inverted handshake, covering Kang's thumb with his fingers.

177

WRIST GRAB

1: Kang grabs Master Lee's right wrist.

2: Master Lee flexes his arm at the elbow, loops his hand counterclockwise, and grabs Kang's hand.

3: He grabs Kang's wrist with his left hand and, with a top block catch, swings it downward and counterclockwise. Master Lee catches it with his right hand in an inverted handshake, covering Kang's thumb with his fingers.

CHOKE

1: Kang chokes Master Lee from the front.

2: Stepping back with the right foot, Master Lee pulls Kang off-balance while looping his left elbow over and down on Kang's elbow. He grabs Kang's left hand with his right hand in a palm-up position.

3: Holding Kang's left wrist with his right hand, Master Lee swings it downward and counterclockwise. He catches it with his right hand in an inverted handshake, covering Kang's thumb with his fingers.

REAR SHOULDER GRAB

1: Kang grabs Master Lee's shoulder from behind.

2: Master Lee spins on his left foot, trapping Kang's grabbing hand with his right hand. He breaks Kang's grip by looping his left arm clockwise over the hand.

3: Once he gains control of Kang's left hand, Master Lee swings it downward and counterclockwise with his grip over Kang's palm.

KNIFE ATTACK

1: Kang threatens Master Lee with an overhead knife attack.

2: As Kang attacks, Master Lee deflects the blow with his left palm while sidestepping and catches Kang's hand with a top block catch.

3: He wrenches Kang's arm around counterclockwise, placing him in the precursor position for a reverse S-lock.

STAGE II: SETUP AND TAKEDOWN
VARIATION 1: REVERSE S-LOCK SHOULDER THROW

At this point, your shoulder is already under your opponent's armpit—a perfect position for a shoulder throw, which should be your first takedown choice. In this position, there is immense torque on your opponent's shoulder, and he will do anything to try to straighten his arm. If you have the proper pressure on his joints, this should not happen. If your opponent somehow manages to straighten his arm, however, there is nothing to worry about because you can then execute a standard shoulder throw.

Be sure your hip position is correct, maintain the counter-pressure on his elbow and hand, and simply press up with your legs and bend forward at your waist to execute the throw. As long as you have constant pressure pushing outward on his elbow, your opponent will not be able to turn in and escape.

1: Master Lee places his left forearm in the crook of Kang's elbow and bends the arm.

2: He pivots on his right foot and places his right shoulder under Kang's armpit while maintaining the angle of the wrist and elbow.

3: Master Lee bends over and sends Kang hurtling over his shoulder. (Note that, by pulling straight down, one can easily dislocate the shoulder, and ideally the shoulder will be pulled out of joint before your opponent hits the ground.)

VARIATION 2: WRIST-CRANK SHOULDER DRAG

This technique can be applied when the control of his elbow with your left hand is compromised. At that point, take your left hand and place it over your right hand, pulling downward with both hands while pinning your opponent's elbow against your shoulder and chest.

By dropping down with your knee on the same side as his arm, you will throw your opponent's weight forward. Continue to drive and drag your right shoulder all the way to the ground, never letting pressure off his wrist.

1: Master Lee places his left forearm in the crook of Kang's elbow and bends the arm.

2: He pivots on his right foot and places his right shoulder under Kang's armpit while maintaining the angle of the wrist and elbow.

3: Master Lee releases the elbow with his right hand and grabs the top of Kang's hand, bending the wrist. He kneels and pulls Kang forward.

STAGE III: GROUND LOCKUP
VARIATION 1: KNEE-ON-NECK REVERSE QUICK C-LOCK

As soon as your opponent lands in front of you, place your right knee on his shoulder and chest, pinning his left shoulder to the ground. Allow the line from the opponent's elbow to his fingertips to straighten, reach under his hand with your left hand in a palm-up position, and twist to acquire the reverse C-lock position. Bring your left leg in and around the elbow to trap it between your legs. Continue to torque on the hand for a wrist dislocation. Should your

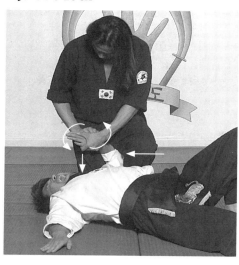

opponent muscle his way out of the grip, this is still a perfect position to transition into a standard armbar.

1: When Kang lands, Master Lee maintains control of his wrist and elbow.

2: He reaches under Kang's hand with his left hand.

3: Master Lee pins Kang's shoulder with his right knee while holding Kang's elbow between his knees. He applies pressure to the wrist with a reverse C-lock.

VARIATION 2: WRIST CRANK WITH SHOULDER QUICK LOCK

In order for this technique to work, do not release the opponent's arm; for the wrist crank to work, control over his wrist cannot be compromised. With this criteria met, it is easy to finish with the wrist crank.

Place your body weight on his shoulder with your shoulder, pinning it on the ground. Continue to pull his hand up in the wrist-crank position, or use the ground by holding the opponent's hand in place and pushing your chest downward onto his elbow, creating extreme compression of the wrist. Your shoulder pins his elbow while either your hands or the ground pin his hand.

1: Master Lee releases the elbow with his right hand and grabs the top of Kang's hand, bending the wrist. He kneels and pulls Kang forward.

2: Master Lee drives his shoulder downward, and Kang tumbles over.

3: With Kang's elbow pinned against Master Lee's shoulder and chest, he presses downward with his torso and pulls Kang's wrist toward him with both hands, securing the painful wrist lock.

CHAPTER 12

ARMBARS   p'alkumch'i kkokki   팔굼치꺽기

KNIFEHAND ARMBAR   k'al nogi   칼넣기

EXPLANATION

The knifehand armbar is very common, but so are the mistakes in its execution. The concept is very simple—keep the arm straight and apply pressure against the joint of the elbow—however, the knifehand armbar is not very secure as a finishing technique and can be relatively easy to counter. This is why it is a good setup technique for other locks.

KEY POINTS TO ENHANCE EFFECTIVENESS
STAGE I: ACQUIRING THE GRIP AND ANGLE

Grab your opponent's right hand and twist clockwise to expose his elbow. A common mistake occurs while applying pressure to the elbow. Do not apply the knifehand to the elbow itself; instead, apply it just above the elbow to the triceps tendon.

PUNCH

1: Kang prepares to strike Master Lee.

2: As Kang punches, Master Lee responds with a right outward knifehand block while sidestepping to the left.

3: He pivots and applies a standing armbar with an outside/inside catch.

LAPEL GRAB

1: Kang grabs Master Lee's lapel and prepares to strike.

2: Master Lee turns his body to the left to minimize the exposed surface area and grabs Kang's wrist with his right hand.

3: He turns Kang's wrist clockwise and applies a standing armbar.

WRIST GRAB

1: Kang grabs Master Lee's right wrist with his right hand and prepares to strike him.

2: Master Lee steps to the left and circles his hand clockwise over Kang's hand.

3: Master Lee continues the clockwise motion and applies the standing armbar.

CHOKE

1: Kang chokes Master Lee from the front.

2: Master Lee steps back with his left foot and reaches over with his right hand to grab Kang's right palm.

3: He turns Kang's wrist and pushes against his elbow to create a standing armbar.

REAR SHOULDER GRAB

1: Kang grabs Master Lee's shoulder from behind.

2: Master Lee spins on his right foot and traps Kang's hand with his right hand.

3: Master Lee cranks Kang's arm and wrist clockwise and administers a standing armbar.

KNIFE ATTACK

1: Kang menaces Master Lee with a knife.

2: As Kang thrusts, Master Lee deflects the attack with his left hand and covers with his right hand, using a cross-down block catch.

3: He twists Kang's wrist with his right hand and administers a standing armbar.

IMPORTANT THINGS TO REMEMBER

1. Remember to keep the elbow straight.

2. Make sure that you have the proper grip on the hand and control the direction of the elbow. A common mistake occurs when people grip the wrist rather than the hand. Gripping the wrist offers no leverage, and the opponent can easily turn his elbow at a whim. By properly controlling the hand, however, he cannot turn his elbow as easily owing to the additional tension put on the wrist when he attempts to counter.

3. Again, remember to apply downward pressure to the triceps tendon, slightly above the elbow, rather than to the elbow itself.

4. Rather than use the palm of your hand, use the blade edge of your wrist (the ulna) to apply pressure against his triceps tendon. This guarantees pain compliance.

5. Lift your opponent's hand with your right hand while applying constant pressure downward on the elbow. If you fail to do this, the technique will make no use of the fulcrum and lever principles, and it will be ineffective.

STAGE II: SETUP AND TAKEDOWN

After you've stepped through with your left foot to acquire the armbar, throw your opponent off-balance so he folds at his waist. Take one more step forward with your right foot and drop to your left knee. Continue to drive your left knifehand into the pressure point slightly above the elbow while lifting up on his hand.

1: Master Lee steps through with his left leg while exerting pressure on Kang's elbow and lifting his wrist.

2: With Kang's arm locked in the armbar, Master Lee takes a step forward with his right foot and lowers his stance.

3: He drops to the one-knee position and uses the armbar to force Kang to the ground.

STAGE III: GROUND LOCKUP
VARIATION 1: KNEE-ON-BACK SHOULDER LOCK

As soon as your opponent falls to the ground, place your knee on his shoulder blade and pin his shoulder to the ground while trapping his hand on the inner thigh of your right leg. Maintain pressure on the elbow at all times.

After you've secured this position, a shoulder dislocation is relatively simple. Push your hips forward and walk toward his head, and the shoulder will dislocate with ease.

1: Master Lee pulls Kang's arm to the side and pushes his shoulder firmly to the ground, then slides his left knee onto Kang's shoulder blade.

2: Master Lee dislocates Kang's shoulder by trapping his wrist against his inner thigh, pinning the shoulder with his left knee, and maintaining pressure on the elbow while moving forward.

VARIATION 2: ARMBAR WITH STOMACH

This technique is an excellent submission. Lean your body weight onto your opponent's shoulder and back, pinning him to the ground with your left side. With your left elbow, push his face away to elongate his arm and give him less room to move. Slide your right leg up so his wrist is pinned on top of your right thigh. Keep your right knee bent to prevent possible escape.

Next, crunch forward at the waist, making sure his elbow is trapped and pressed across your stomach. You can have his elbow higher up on your chest, but it is much more effective when his elbow is lower on your body near the stomach.

1: Continuing the forward momentum, Master Lee uses his left arm as a base and pulls Kang's arm into his midsection, maintaining constant pressure on the elbow.

2: Master Lee places Kang's wrist on top of his right thigh, trapping the hand, then slides his left leg through to tighten the hold. He then crunches his stomach forward, placing immense pressure on the elbow.

TOP SHOULDER ARMBAR   okkae golki   어깨걸기

EXPLANATION

The top shoulder armbar works the same as any other armbar—by placing pressure against the elbow joint. Here, we use the top of the shoulder as the fulcrum to do so. This is a strong leverage technique used for dislocation, but there is minimal containment of the elbow. Therefore, it is imperative that you do not lose the grip on the hand. As long as you maintain control of your opponent's hand, many other techniques are available should his elbow escape.

KEY POINTS TO ENHANCE EFFECTIVENESS
STAGE I: ACQUIRING THE GRIP AND ANGLE

After gripping the opponent's hand, slip your shoulder under the elbow joint as soon as possible to avoid retraction of the arm. The biceps is a strong muscle, and if there is space or the pressure on the elbow is weak, your opponent might bend his arm. There are other counters to attack the shoulder should this occur, but trying to straighten the arm once it is bent is futile.

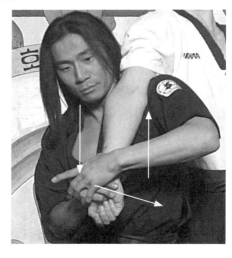

Be sure to place your shoulder under the elbow and not under the armpit. Raising your left arm high in the air will cause the elbow to slip down to the top shoulder position. Clamp down on the opponent's wrist, and press up with your legs and stand straight while pulling down and inward on the opponent's hand and wrist. With the proper force, your opponent will not be able to turn into you to grab or strike with the other hand.

A common mistake with this technique occurs when the elbow is not properly set on the shoulder. This can be prevented by making sure you have firm control of his hand and his palm is facing upward, with his elbow pointing down in the top shoulder position.

PUNCH

1: MacKnight prepares to strike Master Lee.

2: As he punches, Master Lee sidesteps to the left and hooks the wrist with his right hand using an outside soft block.

3: Stepping through with his left foot, Master Lee presses upward against MacKnight's elbow with the top of his shoulder.

LAPEL GRAB

1: MacKnight grabs Master Lee's lapel and prepares to strike.

2: Master Lee sidesteps to the left, pulling MacKnight off-balance and loosening his grip, and grabs MacKnight's hand with his right hand.

3: Stepping through with his left foot, Master Lee presses upward against MacKnight's elbow with the top of his shoulder.

193

WRIST GRAB

1: MacKnight grabs Master Lee's right wrist with his right hand.

2: He steps to the right, pulling MacKnight forward, and grabs MacKnight's wrist with his right hand.

3: Stepping through with his left foot, Master Lee presses upward against MacKnight's elbow with the top of his shoulder.

CHOKE

1: MacKnight chokes Master Lee with both hands.

2: Master Lee steps back, pulling MacKnight off-balance, and grabs MacKnight's right wrist with his right hand and lifts his left arm above his head.

3: With a quick weaving motion, Master Lee ducks between MacKnight's arms and, while retaining control of the wrist, presses upward against MacKnight's right elbow with the top of his left shoulder.

REAR SHOULDER GRAB

1: MacKnight grabs Master Lee's shoulder from behind and prepares to strike.

2: Pivoting on his right foot, Master Lee pushes MacKnight's hand off with his left hand while capturing it with his right.

3: He slides in with his right foot and presses upward against MacKnight's elbow with the top of his shoulder.

KNIFE ATTACK

1: MacKnight threatens Master Lee with a knife.

2: As MacKnight lunges, Master Lee sidesteps and parries with his left palm while capturing the wrist with his right hand.

3: With MacKnight's hand in a palm-up position, Master Lee presses upward against the elbow with the top of his shoulder.

STAGE II: SETUP AND TAKEDOWN
VARIATION 1: SHOULDER THROW

After the opponent's elbow is secured in the top shoulder position, applying the shoulder throw is easy. Maintain constant pressure on the elbow, and slide your shoulder back to the opponent's armpit while pulling his arm forward. Once your shoulder is firmly in place underneath his armpit, pull his arm down and across your body to your right side while simultaneously straightening your legs and bending forward at the waist.

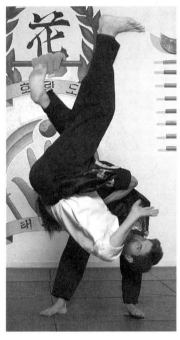

Keep your hip out to the left side to completely block the opponent's hips and secure the throw. Also, make sure to keep your grip on the opponent's hand during the throw in order to quickly lock him up on the ground. You might decide to release your left hand on the opponent's wrist and move it to his shoulder for better control during the throw.

1: By extending his left arm over his head, Master Lee secures MacKnight's upper arm between his neck and shoulder.

2: He pulls down on the wrist with both hands, increasing the pressure on MacKnight's elbow and lifting him to his toes.

3: With a simple bowing motion, Master Lee performs the shoulder throw.

VARIATION 2: ELBOW DRAG FORWARD SWEEP

This technique can be applied when the opponent's elbow slips off the top shoulder position. You can also purposely slide his elbow off your shoulder to set up this take-down. Maintain constant pressure against his elbow joint and drive your weight downward by bending forward at the waist, keeping your head down, and pull his arm across your body to the right side. Simultaneously, sweep his right leg by the knee with an outside sweep.

1: By extending his left arm over his head, Master Lee secures MacKnight's upper arm between his neck and shoulder.

2: He pulls down on the wrist with both hands, increasing the pressure on MacKnight's elbow and lifting him to his toes.

3: Master Lee slides his left leg back against MacKnight's knee and checks it while leaning forward and pulling the wrist across his chest.

STAGE III: GROUND LOCKUP
VARIATION 1: SHIN-ON-ELBOW QUICK LOCK

After the shoulder throw, your opponent will land directly in front of you with his arm extended, which is ideal for the shin-on-elbow quick lock.

1: As MacKnight falls, Master Lee keeps his arm straight by controlling the wrist and elbow.

2: He pulls the arm over MacKnight's head while keeping the palm on the floor.

3: To finish, Master Lee drops his right shin on MacKnight's elbow while pulling up on the wrist with both hands, using a shin-on-elbow quick lock.

VARIATION 2: ARMBAR WITH STOMACH

After landing on the ground, press your shoulder up tightly against the opponent's upper arm. Extend your left arm over the opponent's for better support, and slide his elbow down to your stomach, maintaining constant pressure on the elbow with your torso.

Place his hand, with the palm down, on top of your right thigh as you slide your right leg in higher and closer to the opponent. At the same time, pull his wrist down and trap it with your hip joint as you crunch downward with your stomach, hyperextending his elbow.

1: After administering the elbow drag forward sweep, Master Lee drops his shoulder into MacKnight's arm near the triceps while pulling it straight.

2: He reaches over and establishes a stable base with his left arm.

3: Master Lee finishes by bracing the wrist on top of his right thigh and dropping his stomach and chest down and through MacKnight's elbow.

ARMPIT ARMBAR   p'alkumch'i gama kkokki
팔굼치감아꺽기

EXPLANATION

The armpit armbar is one of the most effective stand-up armbar applications. It allows you to maintain a tight grip on the arm with both hands,
while your triceps and latissimus dorsi clamp tightly on the opponent's arm,
offering additional control and containment to finalize the lock. This is a
great technique for transitioning into other locks, but it is also very effective as a stand-alone technique to defend, take down and submit.

Because this armbar is commonly misunderstood, however, I will specify
what *not* to do:

1. Do not release the grip with either hand.

2. Do not strike at the opponent's elbow with a knifehand or with your
own elbow by lifting the elbow up, creating space, then striking down.

3. Remember that this is an armbar, not a wrist crank. Do not try to
apply excessive force to bend the wrist backward. The purpose of keeping
the opponent's wrist bent is to control and contain his elbow.

With these "don'ts" in mind, we can apply the armpit armbar.

KEY POINTS TO ENHANCE EFFECTIVENESS
STAGE I: ACQUIRING THE GRIP AND ANGLE

The effectiveness
of this technique is
based on the oppo-
nent's elbow being
trapped firmly under-
neath your armpit. As
you trap it and force
your opponent to
bend down, he will
respond by trying
to pull his arm up,
which will cause it to
be secured even more
tightly.

PUNCH

1: MacKnight threatens Master Lee.

2: As MacKnight strikes, Master Lee parries the punch with a right palm while sidestepping to the right.

3: While maintaining control of MacKnight's hand, Master Lee reaches up and grabs his wrist with his left hand, acquiring a hand-and-wrist grip.

LAPEL GRAB

1: MacKnight grabs Master Lee's lapel and prepares to strike him.

2: Master Lee steps back with his left foot and reaches over MacKnight's hand with his right hand.

3: While maintaining control of MacKnight's hand, Master Lee reaches up and grabs his wrist with his left hand, acquiring a hand-and-wrist grip.

WRIST GRAB

1: MacKnight grabs Master Lee's left wrist with his right hand.

2: Master Lee drops back and pulls MacKnight off-balance while reaching across and grabbing the wrist with his right hand.

3: Master Lee twists MacKnight's wrist and forearm clockwise while grabbing the wrist with his left hand, attaining the hand-and-wrist grip.

CHOKE

1: MacKnight chokes Master Lee with both hands.

2: Master Lee reaches over both arms with his right hand and grabs MacKnight's right hand.

3: Master Lee grabs MacKnight's right wrist with his left hand. He pivots on his left foot and bends MacKnight's wrist while wrenching the arm clockwise, forcing him to release his grip.

REAR SHOULDER GRAB

1: MacKnight grabs Master Lee's shoulder from behind.

2: Master Lee spins on his right foot and grabs MacKnight's hand with his right hand.

3: Master Lee grabs MacKnight's right wrist with his left hand. He pivots on his left foot and bends MacKnight's wrist while wrenching the arm clockwise, forcing him to release his grip.

KNIFE ATTACK

1: MacKnight threatens Master Lee with a knife.

2: As MacKnight thrusts, Master Lee blocks with his left hand and grabs the wrist with his right hand, using a cross-down block catch.

3: Master Lee bends the wrist and twists the hand, ensuring that the blade is pointed upward, and wrenches the arm clockwise.

IMPORTANT THINGS TO REMEMBER

1. Keep your back straight and do not crouch. Lower your body by assuming a secure horse stance, then squatting down.

2. Remember that the hand controls the wrist and that the wrist controls the elbow. Therefore, wherever the opponent's fingers are made to point is also the direction where the elbow will point. When you are breaking the elbow from the stand-up position, point the opponent's fingers to the outside, away from you. Pull his elbow in toward your body by pinching in with your left upper arm while twisting his wrist away from you. When you want to take the person down, merely reposition the fingers to point upward so the elbow is also pointing up.

3. Make sure the movements are done smoothly without any jerking motion.

STAGE II: SETUP AND TAKEDOWN
VARIATION 1: ARMPIT-ARMBAR TAKEDOWN

Use your right hand to ensure that the opponent's fingers are pointing up, and press downward with your left shoulder. By stepping out with your left leg and turning your torso into the opponent's upper arm, you can place your entire body weight on the opponent's arm. At the same time, bridge your back and lift the opponent's hand with your right hand and his wrist with your left hand. Continually drive your weight downward until your opponent goes to the ground with you on his back.

1: Master Lee steps through with his left foot and loops his left arm over MacKnight's, trapping the elbow under his armpit.

2: Making sure to point MacKnight's fingers and elbow upward, Master Lee kicks out his left leg and drops his weight on MacKnight's elbow while pulling up on the wrist for greater leverage.

3: Master Lee lands supine, pinning MacKnight on the floor.

VARIATION 2: BODY-SCISSOR TAKEDOWN

This technique can be applied if the control of your opponent's arm is compromised or if he overpowers you while you were attempting to fold him at the waist.

Release his wrist with your left hand and reach across to the far side of his neck. Obtain a hold on his trapezius with your fingers and pull down, then jump into the opponent's midsection, with your left leg kicking backward in front of the stomach and your right leg kicking forward from behind the opponent's knee. Continue to twist your body counterclockwise, and make sure your opponent falls to his back.

1: Master Lee steps through with his left foot and loops his left arm over MacKnight's, trapping the elbow under his armpit.

2: When he is overpowered, Master Lee keeps the wrist locked to prevent MacKnight from countering, and he grabs his neck.

3: Master Lee pulls himself into MacKnight and throws his left leg in front of his stomach and his right leg behind his legs, scissoring him to the floor.

STAGE III: GROUND LOCKUP
VARIATION 1: SHOULDER LOCK FROM REAR UPPER-SIDE MOUNT POSITION

This is a submission technique. After the takedown, quickly place your left hand on your opponent's elbow and your elbow on the pressure point at the rear fold of his shoulder. Move your hip and body

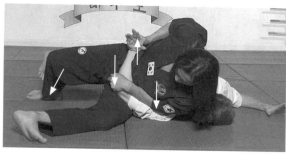

farther up onto the opponent's back.

Pull his arm across your stomach, and trap his wrist in the fold of your hip joint. Slide your right hip up toward his head by pushing off your right leg while pressing down on his shoulder with your left elbow. Make sure to raise your hip off the ground to deliver your full body weight into the torque on the opponent's shoulder.

1: Master Lee pushes down on MacKnight's shoulder blade with his elbow and secures MacKnight's elbow with his left hand.

2: He repositions his body weight and leans into MacKnight.

3: Making sure that MacKnight's arm is secure across his midsection and bent at the elbow, Master Lee puts tremendous pressure on the shoulder by pinning it and lifting his right hip toward MacKnight's head.

VARIATION 2: KNEE-BAR SUBMISSION

After landing from the body-scissor takedown, quickly reach over and grab hold of your opponent's leg by his ankle and calf. Move your left leg over the opponent's right leg and tuck your feet near the opponent's buttocks (to prevent him from catching your leg). Hug his lower leg tightly with both arms for greater leverage, bringing his leg to your left side or to the upward position. Now you are ready to bridge your body. This will dislocate his knee by applying pressure against it with your hips.

As a transitional technique, you can pin the opponent's left leg with your left side and strike to his groin with your right heel a few times before applying the knee bar. Additionally, you can move your opponent's right foot under your left armpit for an even tighter knee-bar position.

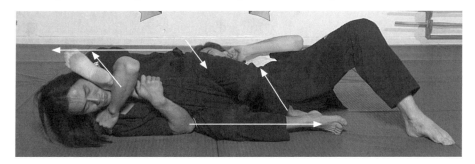

1: After the takedown, Master Lee prepares to turn into MacKnight's legs.

2: He swings his left leg and left arm over MacKnight's leg, securing the knee between his thighs.

3: Hugging the lower leg tightly with both hands and arching his back, Master Lee finishes with the knee bar.

LEG ARMBAR   *p'alkumch'i darigolki*   팔굼치다리걸기

EXPLANATION

The leg armbar applies the same leverage on the elbow joint, but with the legs. This is a very powerful technique because the legs are much larger and stronger than the arm. The dislocation of the elbow is easily accomplished with this hold, so you must pay close attention to safety until you gain a sense of how much force needs to be applied without causing a full dislocation. To apply this technique, trap the opponent's arm by the elbow between both of your legs, then move them in opposite directions to dislocate the elbow.

KEY POINTS TO ENHANCE EFFECTIVENESS
STAGE I: ACQUIRING THE GRIP AND ANGLE

First, acquire the hand-and-wrist grip and keep the opponent's arm straight. The opponent's fingers should once again be turned to the side rather than straight up. The leg armbar is achieved by raising your leg high into the air and dropping it on the elbow with an ax kick. You can also do this with an inside crescent kick, but I believe the ax kick is more powerful.

After dropping your leg, make sure that the opponent's fingers are pointing away from you. To dislocate the elbow, simultaneously push back with your left leg and forward with your right.

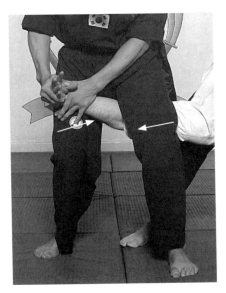

PUNCH

1: MacKnight prepares to strike Master Lee.

2: As MacKnight punches, Master Lee steps in with his left foot and blocks the punch with an inside soft block.

3: He swings the arm down in a clockwise loop and captures the hand with his right hand using a modified cross-down block catch.

LAPEL GRAB

1: MacKnight grabs Master Lee's lapel and prepares to strike him.

2: Master Lee responds by stepping back with his right foot while swinging his left forearm down on MacKnight's right wrist, loosening his grip.

3: Master Lee continues to swing his arm in a clockwise loop and catches MacKnight's hand in his right hand.

WRIST GRAB

1: MacKnight grabs Master Lee's left wrist with his right hand.

2: Master Lee twists his arm counterclockwise and catches MacKnight's wrist between his left thumb and index finger.

3: He reaches over with his right hand and grabs the top of MacKnight's hand while his left hand maintains control of the wrist.

CHOKE

1: MacKnight chokes Master Lee with both hands.

2: Master Lee twists his body to the left while stepping back, pulling MacKnight off-balance. He reaches over MacKnight's arms with his right hand and grabs MacKnight's right hand while grabbing the right wrist with his left hand.

3: Shifting his weight to the right, Master Lee whips MacKnight's arm in a clockwise loop while bending the wrist.

REAR SHOULDER GRAB

1: MacKnight grabs Master Lee's shoulder from behind.

2: Master Lee spins on his right foot and traps MacKnight's wrist with both hands.

3: Shifting his weight to the right, Master Lee whips MacKnight's arm in a clockwise loop while bending the wrist.

KNIFE ATTACK

1: MacKnight threatens Master Lee with a knife.

2: As MacKnight thrusts, Master Lee steps to the right and blocks with his left hand while grabbing the wrist with a right cross-down block catch.

3: Twisting the weapon hand so the tip of the blade is pointed upward, Master Lee loops the arm clockwise while bending the wrist.

STAGE II: SETUP AND TAKEDOWN
VARIATION 1: LEG-ARMBAR TAKEDOWN

To take your opponent down from this position is very easy. Simply turn his fingers up with your right hand, which will make his elbow point upward. This will ensure that your opponent is taken down without any chance for him to bend his elbow. Take him down by dropping to your left knee.

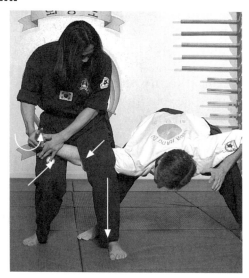

1. With a circling of the arm in a clockwise direction, Master Lee bends MacKnight forward, locking his wrist.

2. Master Lee shoots his leg high into the air.

3. Master Lee brings his leg down over MacKnight's elbow, at which point a possible elbow break can occur.

213

VARIATION 2: LEG-ARMBAR SCISSOR ROLL

This is a great takedown from the leg-armbar position because it transitions into the ground-armbar submission hold. Make sure to have a tight hold on the opponent's arm with both of your arms while your inner thighs and crotch keep in constant contact with the opponent's elbow. Simply drop down and roll to your left shoulder while extending your left leg all the way across the opponent's left foot.

Continue to roll on your left shoulder as you pull back tightly on the opponent's arm while pushing in the opposite direction with your right leg and bridging your body. Your right leg should land across your opponent's chest or stomach.

1: Master Lee shoots his leg high into the air.

2: He drops an ax kick over MacKnight's elbow and locks it between his legs.

3: Master Lee drops his left hand and left knee to the floor, forcing MacKnight down by pulling up on the wrist and pushing down on the elbow with his hips.

STAGE III: GROUND LOCKUP
VARIATION 1: LEG-ARMBAR SUBMISSION

After your opponent drops to the ground, sit back into the OKP as you lift the opponent's hand with your right hand and trap it on top of your right thigh. For additional pressure on the elbow, drive your right knee inward.

At the same time, reach over with your free left hand under his chin and across the neck. Grip his windpipe with your fingers, making sure to keep your fingers away from his mouth to avoid being bitten. Once the grip has been established, pull the opponent's windpipe in the opposite direction of his extended arm. This should suffice as a submission. Your opponent will be on one knee, which might allow him to push off with his legs to try to roll out. However, if you control his head by holding his throat, it will be difficult for him to roll.

To flatten out your opponent, pull up on his arm and sit back farther, placing your weight over his back while bridging your hips forward.

1: Master Lee drops his left knee to the ground and presses down on MacKnight's elbow with his left thigh and buttocks, forcing him to the ground.

2: Pulling up on MacKnight's wrist, he increases the pressure on the elbow, forcing his face into the ground.

3: Master Lee reaches with his left hand under MacKnight's chin and pulls up on his throat, twisting his neck, elbow and shoulder.

VARIATION 2: GROUND-ARMBAR SUBMISSION

Here, simply finish with the classic ground armbar.

1: Holding the arm securely, Master Lee rolls over his left shoulder while hooking upward with his right leg and blocking MacKnight's left foot with his left foot.

2: Master Lee flips MacKnight over.

3: Master Lee lands in a perfect armbar position.

GLOSSARY

aikido 아이키도 合氣道 – (lit. "way of harmonious energy") Japanese martial art founded by Morihei Uyeshiba, based predominantly on joint-manipulation and throwing techniques. Widely practiced around the world, *aikido* has splintered into many variants, some of which bear little resemblance to the original methods of the founder. Moriteru Uyeshiba, the founder's grandson, is aikido's current leader as of this writing.

chiap sul 지압술 指壓術 – the art and science of acupressure

ch'imgu sul 침구술 針灸術 – the art and science of acupuncture and moxibustion

ch'oe-myon sul 최면술 催眠術 – the art and science of hypnotism

Choi, Yong-Sul 최용술 崔龍述 (Yong-Sul, Yong-Sool) – Korean student of daito-ryu aiki-jujutsu headmaster Takeda Sokaku. Credited with bringing the body of knowledge to Korea that eventually became hapkido. His early teachings were referred to as *yusul* (the Korean pronunciation of jujutsu).

chongdo 정도 正道 – (lit. "true way" or "straight path") aspiration of the Hwarang warrior to always follow the right path, even when it may be far more difficult than a less scrupulous path

Choson 조선 朝鮮 (1392-1910) – the last of the Korean dynasties, founded by Yi Song-gye in 1392. Yi established Confucianism as the state doctrine, thus disenfranchising the Hwarang institution and leading to the decline of martial artistry in Korea.

chung ki 중기 重氣 – rooting techniques designed to make the practitioner's body seem very heavy or immovable

Chung-guk Kuksul Shipp'algi 중국국술 십팔기 中國國術十八技
– (lit. "Chinese National Art of 18 Techniques") The formal name for Chinese martial arts as practiced in Korea after the liberation from Japan. The term "18 Techniques" refers to the teachings of certain Shaolin-based systems that supposedly can be broken into 18 categories. According to some practitioners and instructors, the Chinese martial arts that were taught in Korea at the time were praying mantis, baguazhang, or northern Shaolin. See also **kuksul**.

chu sul 주술 呪術 – the art and science of using chanting and intonation techniques as a means of healing disease

ch'yol ki 철기 鐵氣 – body-toughening techniques, based on *ki* manipulation and cultivation exercises, that enable one to withstand incredible impact and stress to the body without harm

chyopkol sul 접골술 接骨術 – the art and science of bone setting

daito-ryu aiki-jujutsu 대동류합기유술 大東流合氣柔術
– (lit. "great Eastern school of harmonious energy soft art") Japanese martial art taught by Takeda Sokaku that later became the basis of aikido and *hapkido*. While including some percussive techniques, this art centers primarily on locking, throwing and pinning techniques and emphasizes the *aiki* concept of using an opponent's momentum against him.

daito-ryu jujutsu – See **daito-ryu aiki-jujutsu.**

daito-ryu yawara – See **daito-ryu aiki-jujutsu.**

-dosa 도사 道師 – (lit. "teacher of the way") Korean term for a wandering monk who is schooled in Buddhism or Taoism. While the "do" prefix alludes to a Taoist background, the "way" spoken of in this context is an understanding of both Buddhism and Taoism—Buddhism for its religious doctrine, and Taoism for its philosophy.

Hanguk Mudo Hoi 한국무도회 韓國武道會 – Korean Martial Art Association. Note that this is an entirely different governing body than the Taehan Mudo Hoi.

hap 합 合 – harmony, combination, aggregation; one of the three *um* elements

hapkido 합기도 合氣道 – (lit. "way of harmonize energy") Korean martial art that evolved from the teachings of Choi Yong-Sul. The Chinese characters are the same as those used for "aikido." Originally, this system had little in the way of percussive technique and no prearranged forms, but a number of Choi Yong-Sul's Korean students claim to have added a variety of techniques from different sources to create the modern variants of hapkido.

hapkido doju 합기도 도주 合氣道道主 – the owner or head authority of the system of hapkido. Choi Yong-Sul was the only one to hold this title undisputedly.

hwa 화 花 – flower

hwa rang do 화랑도 花郎道 – (lit. "way of the flowering noble") comprehensive Korean martial art founded by Dr. Joo Bang Lee in 1960, based on the Hwarang-based system that he learned from Su-Am Dosa. This system includes both traditional Korean martial arts and traditional Korean healing arts.

hwal bop 활법 活法 – special first-aid techniques mainly designed to resuscitate, revive or restore someone injured in combat

Hwarang 화랑 花郎 – (lit. "flowering noble") a young man of noble birth picked to participate in the Silla kingdom's elite warrior corps

Hwarang musul 화랑무술 花郎武術 – blanket term for martial arts practiced by any of the Hwarang regiments. Note that no standardized martial arts curriculum existed at the time, in the same way that it is for the armed forces today.

Hwarang-do 화랑도 花郎徒 – (lit. "flowering noble disciples") See **rangdo**.

im chon mu t'oe 임전무퇴 臨戰無退 – the fourth injunction of the Hwarang, advising them to never retreat in battle

in sul 인술 仁術 (*in sool*) – (lit. "benevolent art") section of hwa rang do's curriculum that centers on healing techniques

in sul 인술 忍術 – the art and science of developing powers of extreme endurance, including pain tolerance, the ability to remain motionless for extended periods of time while stalking a mark, and mental steadfastness in the face of extreme torture. While these sorts of skills seem macabre to the average person, they were utterly crucial to the proper functioning of the Hwarang spy corps. See also **sulsa**.

jujutsu 유술 柔術 – (lit. "soft art") possibly the earliest Japanese martial art. *Jujutsu*, in its earliest manifestations, included striking techniques and a wide variety of joint-manipulation and empty-hand combat techniques. There were many different styles of jujutsu, even in early Japanese history. Also known as *yawara*.

kak 각 角 – (lit. "horn" or "angle") angularity; one of the three *yang* elements

kan 간 間 – distancing or perspective; one of the three yang elements

kang 강 剛 – hard, rigid, strong or tense; one of the three yang elements

kang sul 강술 剛術 – (lit. "hard skills") hard-style techniques that center around the use of straight, linear techniques that are predicated on speed and strength and are usually percussive in nature

Kaya 가야 伽倻 (42-562 A.D.) – a small federation of city-states located between Paekche and Silla; the first to fall to Silla

ki 기 氣 – internal energy, sometimes spoken of as bioelectric or biomagnetic energy

kiryok sul 기력술 氣力術 – the art and science of using the physician's own internal energy as the means of healing a patient

Ko Choson 고조선 古朝鮮 – the first ancient Korean state, formed by the unity of six tribes in the northern part of the Korean peninsula

Koguryo 고구려 高句麗 (37 B.C.-668 A.D.) – Korean kingdom existing during the Three Kingdoms Period; the first to adopt Buddhism from China and the most eager to engage the Chinese armies in battle

kong su do 공수도 空手道 (J. – *karate-do*) – (lit. "way of the empty hand") system of martial arts brought to Korea during the Japanese occupation. By all accounts, the systems practiced in Korea by Japanese soldiers were *shotokan* and/or *shorin-ryu*.

Koryo 고려 高麗 (936-1392 A.D.) – the Korean dynasty that toppled Silla and preceded Choson

kot'ugi 고투기 固鬪技 – the branch of hwa rang do training that deals with ground fighting, submission techniques and grappling strategies

kukson 국선 國仙 (*kuk sun*) – (lit. "national immortal") a high-ranking Hwarang officer, equivalent to the level of general, promoted owing to battlefield excellence as a fighter and leader

kukson-do 국선도 國仙徒 – (lit. "disciples of the national immortal") the Koryo dynasty's name for the Hwarang Corps. See also **rangdo** and **p'ungwol-do**.

Kuksul Hoi 국술회 國術會 – (lit. "National Arts Association") is an abbreviation of *Hanguk Musul Hyophoi* or Korean Martial Arts Association, formed by taking the last syllable in each word

kukup hwal-bop 구급활법 救急活法 – emergency resuscitation techniques

kumdo 검도 劍道 (J. – *kendo*) – fencing system made popular in Korea during the Japanese occupation, wherein armored participants compete against each other using bamboo practice swords

kwan 관 館 – a hall or training hall. In some instances, it describes a style of martial arts practiced by the people from a particular institution, such as *Moo Duk Kwan Tang Soo Do*.

kwon 권 拳 – (lit. "fist") When used as a suffix, this term can signify either a particular hand formation or a complete martial art. For example, *um-yang kwon* is a complete martial art that includes weapons training, ki energy development and acrobatics.

kwonbop 권법 拳法 (C.- *chuan-fa* / *quanfa*, J. – *kenpo*) – (lit. "fist method") a blanket term used to describe fighting techniques, including but not limited to those that incorporate the use of the fist as a weapon

kyo u yi shin 교우이신 交友以信 – the third injunction to the Hwarang, reminding them to conduct themselves in a trustworthy and brotherly manner among friends

kyong ki 경기 輕氣 – agility and energetic training methods designed to make the practitioner's body lighter than normal, allowing him to perform gravity-defying feats

Lee, Joo Bang 이주방 李柱邦 – the founder of hwa rang do

Lee, Joo Sang 이주상 李柱商 – the elder brother of Dr. Joo Bang Lee and the first man to bring hwa rang do to the United States

Lee, Taejoon 이태준 李太準 – the elder son of Dr. Joo Bang Lee

ma ki 마기 麻氣 – techniques and methods to make the body numb or impervious to pain through the use of ki energy

mu do 무도 武道 – (lit. "martial way") nonspecific term for a school or system of martial art training that encompasses combat techniques and the development of one's character (hence the suffix "-do," indicating a "way" of life)

mu sul 무술 武術 – (lit. "martial art") nonspecific term for martial art used in Asian language and literature. In hwa rang do, *mu sul* forms half the curriculum, while *in sul* forms the other half.

mugi gong 무기공 武器功 – weaponry skills

Muye Dobo T'ongji 무예도보통지 武藝圖譜通誌 – canonical text on Korean martial arts compiled in the early 1700s, during the Choson period

nae gong 내공 內功 – (lit. "internal skills") skills achieved through the development of internal ki energy powers

oe gong 외공 外功 – (lit. "external skills") combative and athletic skills

Paekche 백제 百濟 (18 B.C.-660 A.D.) – one of Korea's Three Kingdoms; made the greatest advances into Japan and established a colony there with strong ties to the Korean peninsula

p'ungwol-do 풍월도 風月徒 – (lit. "disciples of the wind and moon") See also **kukson-do**.

rang 랑 郎 – a title of nobility; a groom or a young man

rangdo 랑도 郎徒 – (lit. "disciples of the nobleman") warrior-disciples of commoner status who were under the command and followed the instructions of the Hwarang leaders

sa chin e hyo 사친이효 事親以孝 – the second of the Hwarang injunctions, reminding them to show filial piety toward their parents and teachers

sa kun e chung 사군이충 事君以忠 – the first of the Hwarang injunctions, commanding them to show supreme loyalty to their lord or king

Saburo, Shinra 신라삼랑 新羅三郎 – the man credited with founding *daito-ryu jujutsu*. His name strongly indicates Korean noble ancestry; Shinra is pronounced "Shilla" in Korean, and the final character *ro* is pronounced *rang* in Korean, indicating a likely Hwarang affiliation.

sal saeng yu t'aek 살생유택 殺生有擇 – the fifth and final of the Hwarang injunctions, admonishing them against indiscriminate killing. This rule is unique in that it is the only one of the five with a decidedly Buddhist tone.

sa-sang bop 사상법 四相法 – the study of the four human constitutional types, revealing patterns in body type, psychology and personality

shin 神 – God-like, mystical. The indigenous Japanese religion, Shinto, uses this character, along with the character for "way," referring to its practice as "the way of the gods." This character is clearly different than that of the "Shin" in "Shilla," which means "new."

shin gong 신공 神功 – mystical skills, or skills that would seem supernatural to an outsider

shin ki 신기 神氣 – mystical energy skills, achieved through powerful focus and concentration

shin-kyon sul 신견술 神見術 – the art and science of mental telepathy and remote viewing

Silla 신라 新羅 (57 B.C.-935 A.D.) – the first kingdom to unify the Korean peninsula. It did so through the military might of the Hwarang Corps. Note that the first character is pronounced as *"shin"* in Korean, Japanese and Chinese, meaning "new." See also **shin.**

Sok-Wang Sa Temple 석왕사 釋旺寺 – the original home of Su-Am Dosa, where the Lee brothers first met their master

Son 선 禪 (J.– *Zen*) – sect of Buddhism that advocates strict training to achieve enlightenment

son hak 선학 禪學 – the study of skills relating to immortality, hermitage, wilderness survival and magic. Through developing greater control of the mind, the ancient Hwarang were able to achieve and wield powers that would be nothing short of sorcery to the commoner.

sonbae 선배 先輩 – the warrior corps of Koguryo

Sonsa 선사 禪師 – a master of Son Buddhism. This term is generally interchangeable with "Dosa" because many mystics in Korea were well-learned in both Buddhist and Taoist scripture, magic and martial arts. See also **Dosa.**

Su-Am Dosa 수암도사 修岩道師 / 禪師 / 仙師 (Su-Ahm Dosa) – the hermit monk who befriended Ha-Young Lee and taught his sons, Joo Bang Lee and Joo Sang Lee, the body of Hwarang knowledge that had been passed on to him. Su-Am Dosa was the 57th inheritor of the Hwarang legacy, which Joo Bang Lee later reorganized and systematized into what is now hwa rang do.

Su-Am Sonsa 수암선사 修岩禪師 – See **Su-Am Dosa** and **Sonsa**.

su-bak 수박 手搏 – a blanket term used to describe unarmed combat, literally meaning "to strike with the hand." Later became used to denote a specific branch of martial art in the 20th century.

sulsa 술사 術師 – ancient Hwarang spies employed for the purposes of espionage, assassination and demolition

T'ae-Guk Um-Yang O-Haeng Bop 태국음양오행법 太極陰陽五行法 – the study of universal laws based on the theory of polar opposites (*um-yang*) and the five elements (wood, metal, fire, water and earth)

t'aek-kyon 택견 – Korean martial art that centers on foot fighting and involves a wide variety of kicks and sweeps. Hand techniques in this system are predominantly open-handed and include soft blocks, chops and palm strikes. Solo forms look similar to *tai chi* exercises, but with fast kicks. Usually practiced with a partner using pre-arranged footwork patterns, similar to the *jinga* of *capoeira*.

tae jang-gun 대장군 大將軍 – high-ranking general

t'ae su do 태수도 太手道 (*tae soo do*) – (lit. "way of the supreme hand") Also referred to as the "way of the warrior spirit," *tae su do* is an introductory-level martial art designed by the World Hwa Rang Do Association to counter the high attrition rate of novice hwa rang do students. It has a belt-ranking system (as opposed to the sash-ranking system of hwa rang do), which leads up to a black belt. After earning a black belt, the student is allowed to join the more rigorous hwa rang do program.

t'ae su do 태수도 跆手道 – the "prototype" name for the martial art that eventually became *tae kwon do*

taedong-ryu hapki yusul 대동류합기유술 – Korean pronunciation of *daito-ryu aiki-jujitsu*.

Taehan Hapkido Hyophoi 대한합기도협회 大韓合氣道協會 – Korean Hapkido Association

Taehan Hwarangdo Hoi 대한화랑도회 大韓花郎道會 – Korean Hwa Rang Do Association, established as the first ever hwa rang do association in Seoul, Korea, by Dr. Joo Bang Lee

Taehan Mudo Hoi 대한무도회 大韓武道會 – Korean Martial Arts Association

tojang 도장 道場 (*dojang*) – (lit. "site of the way") Korean term for a training area that focuses on a particular martial way. The Chinese characters are the same as those used for the Japanese word *dojo*.

tojunim 도주님 道主任 (*dojoonim*) – (lit. "revered master of the way") a standard term in martial arts that uses *do*, meaning "the way." It signifies the main authority in the system and the person who has proprietary rights over the present and future of the system. Because there are lower grandmaster-level rankings in *hwa rang do*, the English translation of this title is "supreme grandmaster."

tokshim sul 독심술 讀心術 – the art and science of reading a person's mental and emotional state

um-yang 음양 陰陽 (*oom-yang*) – Korean pronunciation of the Chinese *yin-yang*. Depicted as a circle bisected with an S-shaped line, um-yang represents the balance of equal and opposite powers in nature. While the Chinese version of this symbol appears in black and white, the Korean version is usually shown in red and blue—the colors on the Republic of Korea's flag.

um-yang kwon 음양권 陰陽拳 – (lit. "yin-yang fist") the term used by Su-Am Dosa for his method of combat skills taught to the Lee brothers, signifying a balanced method of both hard and soft techniques and a reliance on natural principles. In keeping with the Hwarang ideal, um-yang kwon training was geared toward pushing the practitioner well beyond the limits of normal human performance.

un-shin bop 은신법 隱身法 – concealment methods, employing such techniques as disguise, camouflage, hiding and stealth. The goal of this section of hwa rang do training is to become invisible in broad daylight.

won 원 圓 – round, circular; one of three principles of um

yakbang bop 약방법 藥方法 – the art and science of herbal medicine, specifically combining herbs to make a prescription that is made for the specific illness or imbalances of a particular patient

yamato/wa 大和/倭 – arguably the descendants of Paekche royalty who became the progenitors of the Japanese royal line

Yang Mi Am 양미암 陽嵋庵 – the hermitage of Su-Am Dosa near Seoul

yawara 유술 柔術 – See **jujutsu.**

yu 유 流 – flowing, like water; one of the three principles of um

yudo 유도 柔道 – (lit. "soft way") Korean pronunciation of judo

yu-shim bop 유심법 喩心法 – the study of human emotion and thought

yusul 유술 柔術 (*yoo sool, yu sool*) – (lit. "soft art") the Korean version of jujutsu. Following the Japanese occupation of Korea from 1910 to 1945, all yusul practiced in Korea was propagated by students of Choi Yong-Sul. See also **daito-ryu aiki-jujutsu.**

Books & DVDs from
BLACK BELT ®